Farm to Table

Fabulous

Seasonal Entertaining, Cooking & Inspiration

Kimberly Storm Ritter

Great American Publishers

D0879413

Farm to Table

Fabulous

Great American Publishers

171 Lone Pine Church Road • Lena, MS 39094

TOLL-FREE 1.888.854.5954 • www.GreatAmericanPublishers.com

ISBN 978-1-934817-39-1

10 9 8 7 6 5 4 3 2 1
First Edition

by Kimberly Storm Ritter

Design by Nichole Stewart

Contents

Dedication

I'm dedicating this book to the most amazing woman in the world, my mom. She taught me to be a strong, independent woman by being the best role model I could ever imagine. I refer to her often as "my other half" because through the ups and downs of my life (and there have been many) she has always been by my side.

When I became a single mom to my amazing Kaden, Mom was with me in the delivery room. She continues her selfless acts of kindness in my life everyday during countless school activities, baseball games, birthday parties, and, these days, in the kitchen. Without her, I wouldn't be the woman I am today. I am very fortunate and blessed to call her my superhero.

On the next page, is the one recipe that is tried-and-true in our family. It is like liquid gold. It's comfort food any time of the year and will always make you look like a superstar. It is the base for most of my Italian recipes, and before you even start reading my book, you may just want to whip up a batch for the freezer. It is great to defrost and eat with your favorite pasta any night of the week. So here you go—from generations of fine Italian women—from our family to yours.

Mom's Homemade Spaghetti Sauce and Meatballs

Meatballs:

2 to 3 pounds ground beef
¾ cup finely chopped onions
2 to 4 tablespoons parsley
½ cup breadcrumbs
1 teaspoon sweet basil

1 teaspoon oregano
1 to 2 eggs
Salt and pepper to taste
3 to 4 cloves very finely chopped
   fresh garlic, optional

Mixture should not be too dry or too moist. Mix all ingredients together and form medium meatballs.

Sauce:

Olive oil
4 tablespoons chopped parsley
6 large cloves chopped fresh garlic
½ cup chopped onions
4 tablespoons chopped fresh celery leaves
1 teaspoon sweet basil
1 teaspoon oregano

Salt and pepper to taste
Dash rosemary
2 (6-ounce) cans tomato paste
2 (32-ounce) cans tomato purée
2 (32-ounce) cans tomato sauce
2 (32-ounce) cans crushed tomatoes

Lightly cover bottom of a large pot with olive oil. Sauté all ingredients except tomato products over low heat until onions are translucent. Add meatballs and brown on all sides. You may have to do this in batches depending on how many meatballs you make. Add all meatballs back to the pot and add tomato products. Feel free to mix and match the tomato ingredients to make it your own family recipe. Simmer on low for 3 to 4 hours. Serves 4 to 6.

F2T Tip: This may be made in large batches and frozen for the future for making lasagna, stuffed shells, manicotti, basically any Italian dish. Just pop it out of the freezer, defrost, and dinner is served. This is not something you can whip up quickly so you'll be happy you have extra on a cold snowy day or even a warm rainy one.

Foreword

I come from a very small town in Northeastern Pennsylvania called Daleville, named after my great-grandmother. One might assume that would make me Daleville royalty, but I had a very humble upbringing. My grandparents, Margaret and Robert Storm, were farmers—real honest-to-goodness farmers who owned a produce and egg stand on the side of the road. They were kind, honest, hard-working and incredibly family oriented. I am who I am today because of them.

The original farm to table dinners happened in their dining room at a table that spanned the entire length of a space filled with the joy and laughter of almost thirty aunts, uncles, and cousins. Grandma had mismatched dishes, glasses, utensils, chairs, and piano benches, not because it was cool but because it was what she had to accommodate her large family. Well, I guess it was a bit shabby-chic before that was actually a thing.

Some of my fondest memories came from that dining room, that table, that farmhouse. Grandma Storm could create a dinner for thirty out of her garden; now that's farm to table at its best. Of course let's not forget the entertainment. Back then my cousins and I always had some type of song or dance to perform following dinner. These days, we're either at the piano or on the stage performing a lip-sync battle. Little did I know this would be my life's purpose.

Today, I live in that same farmhouse in the country. Although I still host many family dinners there, we also host extraordinary farm to table dinners at our Ritter's Farm Market. It's our philosophy that dinner isn't just about the food. Dinner is about the people, joy, laughter, conversation, love, and entertainment. It's about the experience, and each one is different in its own special way.

I'm getting ahead of myself. How was the Farm to Table Experience created? It started as a love story. I know it sounds a little corny, but it's my true story... my path. I feel that each moment of our life is a stepping stone leading us exactly where we should be. You're reading this book because this is exactly where you're supposed to be. It is my hope you will gain something from it and maybe even be inspired. We learn a little something from each experience. In my experience, when you feel you are doing what God intended for you, it's easy to use everything you learned to help others while finding joy within yourself.

We found each other through our grief...

A Love Story

In 2015, I lost my husband very suddenly and tragically; two months later, on the West Coast, Ian Ritter lost his wife to an illness. We found each other through our grief and became the best of friends. We knew of each other from high school, but other than saying hello in the hallways, I don't think we ever had a conversation. We spoke across the miles at first and for quite sometime.

When Ian moved back to Northeastern Pennsylvania to help his parents, Jim and Liane Ritter, open their second Ritter's Farm Market location, we decided to have dinner. The rest is history.

Anyone who owns their own business can attest to the fact that the hours are very long, and there is very little time for much else. As Ian and I grew closer, I looked for ways to get more involved in the markets in my free time so my son and I could spend more time with him.

Did I mention my most amazing, creative, incredible son, Kaden? Well he's also a very big part of this story. He's the reason I live and breathe. He's the reason I work so hard and try to be a good role model. He's my everything. Kaden is also the best food critic around. He loves to cook as well, but he loves to eat even more.

So Kaden and I would stock shelves in the farm market, sort vegetables, and go out to the cornfields. Heck, Ian's family even let me drive a truck backwards through the cornfield as they handpicked their corn. Sort of a

Just being in the market was inspiring...

"right of passage" to the Ritter's. Talk about taking their life in their hands. You name it and Kaden and I were willing to help. Just being in the market was inspiring—it was truly our happy place. I believe we all found healing through the farm and each other.

Meant to Be

One evening Kaden was having a sleepover with my mom, a.k.a. mom-mom, and Ian and I were closing up the market. It was the height of the season, and the vegetables were so beautiful that I was truly inspired by the smell, the colors, everything. I asked Ian if he would mind if I cooked a few dishes and put them out for samples the next day in the market. Of course he said yes, and that's how our farm to table department began. From that point forward, our farm to table prepared foods were sold by the pound every weekend. I started catering and cooking all the time. It was fun doing something I truly enjoyed on a daily basis. I cooked my little heart out while working as a full-time sales rep during the week. It was busy but very gratifying.

As the weather got colder and the season drew to a close, we brainstormed ideas to keep cooking through the winter, and that is how the Farm to Table Experience was born. Those who know me also know that I am a very spiritual person. As we were brainstorming our ideas, my spiritual advisor said she saw guests sitting at long tables sharing meals, a sense of community, the way things used to be, if you will.

It was in that moment I knew our dinners were meant to be... as if the best moments of my childhood were coming full circle in my adulthood. I could give people the same experience I had growing up—a freshly cooked meal, seated at one long table, laughter, conversations, performances.

We took a leap... a "quit your job and put all your eggs in one basket" kind of leap. I admit to stressing over the decision a bit. I had a very good career. As a single mom, quitting my job seemed like a pretty selfish thing to do. As a matter of fact, I kept asking God and my angels for signs. One day Ian and I took a ride with his dad, Jim, and we were discussing our farm to table future. When I talked about the fear of quitting my job, Ian's dad gave me the best advice ever. He said, "You can be successful at anything if you work hard."

The words resonated with me. I've been working since I was thirteen years old—work ethic has never been an issue with me. After loading the equipment, the man who sold it to us said, "Here, I have something else for you." He handed us a neon sign from an old restaurant. Jim Ritter looked at me and said, "There's your sign!" We laughed most of the way home. Ian and I knew it was meant to be. Today, that sign hangs amongst the branches in our farm to table area.

The Farm to Table Experience

We picked a random date for our first Farm to Table Experience—the weekend before Thanksgiving—and decided to go for it. Ian's parents, Jim and Liane Ritter, gave us their stamp of approval; my mother, Cynthia Kania, rolled up her sleeves in the kitchen; and we started planning. We took reservations so there was very little waste, and we could cook through the winter months. It was also a way to bring people together that would otherwise never meet.

As an interior designer, I draw inspiration from many places. I'm almost trained; to create an inspiration or color board before I even pick up a pencil or sit at a computer to design a space. It's a great way to get excited about a project. Just pick up some foam core or poster board and find images that inspire you. I recommend doing this (even on a small scale) before your dinners to inspire your decor for the room. I will walk you through my ideas and color schemes each month, but feel free to get creative. You can find images online or in magazines. Maybe the color of a crisp green apple is your inspiration. You may be inspired by the way an image makes you feel, like a set table under the stars out of *Country Living* magazine. Whatever makes you feel happy is what you gather for your board.

Building a Space

Because this was to be a space where we wanted people to feel warmth, nostalgia, and like they're dining in our home, we started Ian's parents, Jim and Liane Ritter, gave us their stamp of approval; my mother, Cynthia Kania, rolled up her sleeves in the kitchen; and we started antiquing—lots and lots of antiquing. We were pretty much starting from scratch in a farm market, so we had blank walls and concrete floors. A few months prior, I painted a mural on the walls. We decided to use it as a base to build upon. The mural is quirky, whimsical, and colorful... kind of like us. Could we have painted it neutral and elegant maybe? Yes, but everyone does that and we wanted to be different.

We initially started with one antique oriental carpet (an amazing one that reminded me of my grandma's house), one table, and half of the room decorated.

Within three months, the events grew so large we had to double the size of the space to accommodate our guests. I purchased eight additional carpets from an antique shop going out of business. We found the most amazing tables that were long enough to fit eight people each.

Collecting chairs was quite the adventure. Field's Used Furniture was wonderful, and we found many very cool chairs there, as well as on Craigslist and our local thrift stores. The idea behind the table, chairs, and space in general was shabby-chic, country farmhouse elegant. You get the idea.

As we collected our carpets, tables, and chairs, we searched for candlesticks, china, and utensils. It was truly a treasure hunt. It was a ton of fun introducing Ian to a passion of mine.

Mirrors—old and new—are essential to the space. They give the room depth and literally double, triple—even quadruple—your magic and sparkle. Chandeliers—mismatched, non-electric ones—are perfect to hang from the ceiling for added chicness and elegance. Oddly enough, we found some mirror-type chandeliers at Big Lots of all places.

We wanted to make the room magical before filling it with our new treasures. My idea was to bring the outdoors inside... especially since we were having these dinners in the colder months, which is basically nine months out of the year in Northeastern Pennsylvania. Ian started dragging the biggest tree branches he could find into

> *They give the room depth and literally double your magic and sparkle.*

the space and securing them to the walls and ceiling. Once they were secure, we strung little white lights on each branch, thousands of lights. Magical. (Helpful tip: go LED. It will save you a ton of money in the long run. However, they must be warm LED.) If your space doesn't allow for big tree branches hanging from the walls, throw a few tree branches in a large planting pot to create the same effect.

We also brought in an electric fireplace with a beautiful mantle from Ian's parents and a baby grand piano since Ian James is the most amazing musician on the planet. Although, his parents may say it's a tie between him and his twin brother, Eric, who is also amazingly talented. Seriously, google them and download their albums; they are amazing. This pretty much created the base or the bones of our room. Everything was in its place and now it was time to decorate.

Decorating

We brought the tables back into the space first. We generally leave the middle of the room open for foot traffic and place long tables around the room in a u-formation, making sure our branches create a canopy over the tables. Once your table or tables are in the room, bring in the chairs. The idea is to mismatch—never putting identical chairs next to one another. I really love cane and wicker. To me, it screams farm to table shabby-chic.

Because I wanted this space to be just dripping with magic, it was time for more shopping. I shopped for strings of pearls and sequins. Basically any type of glittery, shimmery string of anything came home with me for my branches.

Another one of my favorite ways to make the branches sparkle is with crystals—fake, real, whatever you can find works. Just throw your strands over the branches and let them hang straight down, almost touching the table. You don't want them hanging in peoples faces, so position them down the center of the tables. You can also find pretty faux crystal garlands that work well.

Magical, majestic, enchanted are just some of the words our guests use to describe the space.

Lanterns with tealights make great decorations that also provide additional light and a bit of outdoor whimsy. You will literally feel as though you are sitting in a tree house. Magical, majestic, enchanted are just some of the words our guests have used to describe the space.

In each chapter, I describe—month by month—how to transform your room for that season or holiday. You'll have a step-by-step plan for how to decorate and how

to cook a farm to table fabulous meal for your celebration. Because we will layer the room for each occasion, the base will never change; we will only add.

Tablescapes

For tables, we will work from the center of the table out. First, decide whether or not you want a runner. I'm drawn to burlap because it's very farm to table looking. Second, I use every candlestick I can get my hands on—silver, white, crystal, glass. I'm talking at least a dozen per table. I'm not typically drawn to gold or brass, but that doesn't mean you can't use whatever you prefer. As for the candles, we'll use whites, off-whites, and creams. You will see that we use color too, at times, to add interest to our tables for certain holidays. I also like to add tealights glass in votives between my taper candles.

Centerpieces generally consist of fresh fruits in vases. Fill them with water and cut the fruit, or place the fruit in whole without water. You'll find suggestions that compliment the menus in each chapter.

For the china, the idea is to mismatch everything while keeping the same pattern at one place setting. In other words, if we use our blue floral patterned china at one seat, then we may put our green leafy-patterned china at the next place setting. We will talk about this in depth later in the book, but this is the basic idea. Each setting for my recipes should have a dinner plate, a salad plate, and a soup bowl.

Next, your wine glasses and water glasses should be full for each guest. For utensils, I like to display a salad fork, dinner fork, butter knife, and soup spoon. I don't typically place an appetizer plate or anything for dessert on the main table. I prefer to encourage guests to mingle upon arrival before finding their place card and settling in for the evening.

Last, let's talk napkins and place cards. Remember, we're building here, so it's not that a patterned napkin won't work. I just like to go neutral on the napkins. White napkins get stained easily, so if you don't like the whole laundry aspect of the aftermath of the dinner party, go with a gray or darker taupe.

Neutral is the way to go with place cards, too, along with a little gemstone for sparkle. If you want to get fancy, this is a good opportunity. I know there will be plenty of people that disagree with me on where to seat your guests, but here's the deal. When I go out with my significant other, I actually like to spend time with him. It's not often in this business that we get time off with a babysitter to enjoy an evening out.

Therefore, I prefer to place people next to the person that accompanies them because that's how I would want to be seated—unless I'm playing matchmaker, of course. I also like to put couples next to each other as opposed to across from one another. Again, Ian and I are what they call "same-siders," meaning that when we go to dinner we always sit on the same side of the table or booth.

Dinner Time

This is the schedule we follow with our dinners, though we have tweaked it several times over the past year and a half when we saw that something wasn't working.

You don't have to be at a wedding to justify a cocktail hour, and it's a great opportunity to allow your guests to settle into the space. You've created a masterpiece, after all, so give them a chance to take it all in. Enjoy watching their reactions as they enter your magical lair. I promise you, it will take their breath away.

It also gives them the chance to have a drink, mingle with the other guests, and partake in your beautiful hors d'oeuvre, table giving you, the host, time to put finishing touches on your meal. In addition to the "wow" factor of your decor, the hors d'oeuvre table sets the tone for the evening. It's the first course people see and taste.

By definition, an hors d'oeuvre is a one-bite item that's either stationary or passed and served prior to a meal. Appetizers, on the other hand, appear as the first course when seated at the table. However, after learning from customer feedback at farm to table dinners, I like to serve my appetizer course on this table.

Where to serve the hor d'oeuvres will depend upon where you prefer the guests to congregate. If you like to have company in your kitchen, or if that's where everyone ends up anyway, then perhaps set the hors d'oeuvres out on your kitchen island or table. I prefer to set this area up in the dining room. It gives guests the opportunity to get to know one another and gives me a little space to work.

I really like to cover this particular table with a white tablecloth and add some burlap and candles to dress it up and give it that shabby-chic look. I use wooden crates draped with burlap to elevate certain areas of the table for platters, giving it some depth.

This is farm to table, so I like to use anything that's in season for the appetizers and hors d'euvre table. I often use gourmet olives, cheeses, and crackers—always in season, always a crowd pleaser. I like to cut a few pieces off the block of cheese and stick a knife in it for people to serve themselves. I use any and every kind of vegetable for color, especially my favorite tri-colored carrots (yes, they actually grow purple carrots) and peppers (red, yellow, orange, purple, green). They look so beautiful on the blank canvas of the white-and-burlap-covered table. Don't forget toothpicks, plates, and napkins so guests may help themselves.

The remainder of your courses, with the exception of dessert, will be served family-style. It encourages people to interact, especially if you have a large crowd. For dishes, use beautiful soup tureens, serving bowls for salad, and platters for your main course from the china you've collected or in mismatched patterns.

Make sure you have any garnishes on the table, such as croutons, cheese, crostini, etc., for your soup. I prefer to dress the salad prior to serving. Otherwise, I think it can get a little cumbersome and messy passing dressing around to your guests. The main course usually consists of a protein, or if you're doing Italian, a casserole dish and one or two sides. I really like the idea of integrating a vegetable and starch into every meal. You'll see this in every menu throughout the book.

It's dessert time. You can see the finish line... The dinner was amazing—magical ambiance, sparkling conversation, and a hostess with the mostest. You're enjoying all of the fabulous compliments after you've spent the entire week cooking, cleaning, and decorating for your guests. All your friends are meshing beautifully. Now it's time for you to relax and enjoy your last course.

Do yourself a favor and get the coffee poised and ready so all you have to do is push a button. We like to display dessert on a separate table along with the coffee, creamer, sugar etc., so guests can get up and stretch their legs. Plating the dessert makes it easy for guests to grab what they like, along with the utensils, and head back to the table. A dessert display can be another way to utilize your creativity.

Once everyone has dessert and coffee in front of them, it's time for what your guests have been waiting for... the entertainment. No one says you have to perform a musical duet like Rosemary Clooney and Bing Crosby in *White Christmas* or a dance number like Fred Astaire and Ginger Rogers in, well, anything. However, this is a really great opportunity to let your guests know that it's time to cut loose or just relax and get to know their hosts.

For Ian and me, this is probably the most fun part of the evening. It's the time where we get to be our most authentic true selves. We don't give much thought to whether people love it or think we're completely nuts. We perform like no one is watching. Isn't that how we should all live each aspect of our lives?

I should back up a little here for a moment and say that when Ian and I first met, we bonded over music, YouTube videos, and dancing. We upgraded to lip-sync battles our first New Year's Eve together. We got all dressed up and entertained one another, even performing for my mom for her birthday on New Year's Day. Jimmy Fallon was our inspiration, and we've been battling it out ever since. It's something for the whole family as Kaden loves to get involved as well. Over time, it became the highlight of our Farm to Table Experience.

Now that you know the history behind our lip-sync battles, it's time to showcase your talent. Perform for your guests like no one is watching. Trust me, if I can perform Janis Joplin in front of seventy people you can totally do this. So what's your talent? Do you sing or play an instrument? We've done really cool medleys at the piano—*Grease* is my fave. Are you funny and want to do a stand-up comedy routine? Do it! Anyone can lip-sync (it requires virtually no talent at all), so you can totally handle this, not to mention that you'll be the coolest couple around.

So now your evening is complete. You've left your guests wanting more. Pour yourself a glass of wine, have a cup of coffee, or climb in bed and sleep for a week. You've just pulled off your very own Farm to Table Experience.

Pick a Date and Send the Invites

Excited? Are you ready to start planning your own Farm to Table Experience? Pick a month, any month. I have twelve months of menus and evenings already planned out detail by detail in the following chapters. We've already hosted them and know they are successful, so what are you waiting for? Start making your invite list because if I can please fifty to seventy guests with absolutely no culinary training, you can totally do this. We'll be with you every detail and step of the way.

I feel like I should tell you... I had never even cooked one homemade soup (unless you count canned Campbell's or Progresso) before I started cooking for our Farm to Table Experience. Never ever. Not one. I also had never made homemade salad dressing. I mean, why bother when we have a perfectly good variety of homemade dressings in our markets and there's Hidden Valley Ranch and Ken's Italian available? Now, a year and a half later, those are my two favorite things to create from scratch.

If you're reading this book because you want to give cooking a try (I know you're not reading it because I'm a *New York Times* best-selling author), you can do this. I've got your back. I've researched, tweaked, combined, revised, and created more recipes than you can ever imagine. I promise you they are the best of the best, and your guests will not be disappointed. You'll soon discover the recipes are not terribly fussy or fancy... they are simply Farm to Table Fabulous!

Winter Wonderland

Baby it's cold outside... especially here in the Northeast. My inspiration for this month's dinner party is the winter landscape. January brings us freezing cold temperatures. However, it also brings a majestic landscape with blankets of freshly fallen snow that sparkles... especially first thing in the morning almost as if God has taken a handful of glitter and scattered it evenly across the landscape. January glistens; it's that simple. It makes one long for comfort food, warm fires, warm drinks, and cozy nooks in which to snuggle up with a warm blanket and a good book. Or in my case, a trashy magazine chock full of the latest celebrity gossip.

As a family, this is our downtime, so we spend much-needed quality time together—the occasional trip to Montage Mountain to ski, breaking out board games, and some old-fashioned sledding. My son generally has lots of new toys following Christmas, and it's really nice to relax in my jammies with a cup of hot chocolate on a snowy day while Kaden plays.

A good old-fashioned winter blues party is a wonderful way to get everyone out of the house celebrating the New Year. In preparation, search for white, silver or crystal half-priced Christmas decorations and stock up on items to create your very own indoor winter wonderland. One cannot go wrong with a beautiful array of every shade of white possible for room decor, and now is the time to get it inexpensively. This will also create the basis of your room decor in which to build upon in future months.

Room Decorations

Carry this magical, wintry theme throughout the rest of the room. If you have a mantle, I suggest the same candlelit theme. Maybe even drape some lovely strands of pearls over the mantle. It's also a very good area to place some additional lighting. Perhaps a lamp on either side. I enjoy the lamps with glass bottoms that allow one to fill them with all sorts of things. In this case, follow the theme of your tablescape. If you've chosen pinecones for the table, then use pinecones in the rest of the room. If you've chosen green apples and cranberries, then let it be that. You get the idea.

A fun project that adds beauty to your room while including the kiddos, is fabric snowflakes. Think the paper snowflakes we all created as children but with a bit more style. Decorate your space days in advance so your time is completely free to create in the kitchen. Making as much ahead of time as possible also allows you to be farm to table fabulous for your guests.

Tablescape

This month we will use lots of sparkle. The more the merrier. Think dripping with jewels. One strand at a time, dangle strings of sequins, pearls, and crystals from the tree branches already placed in your room. The white lights you've already strung throughout the trees will create an illusion of depth and shimmer from the reflection of light.

Once your guests take in the initial awe of the magic you've created over their heads, they will most certainly be curious to see what is placed in front of them for the evening. My advice, mix and match absolutely everything while keeping it simply elegant. The center of your tables this month will feature as much white as possible.

Break out your white, crystal, and silver mismatched shabby-chic candlesticks paired with candles that are white, off-white. and cream. Don't forget the tea lights. They are inexpensive and may be placed in almost anything. For January, we'll place them down the center of the table, as many as can fit. I suggest keeping the centerpieces simple. Skipping the flower arrangements will leave space for food. (If you decide to use flowers, keep them elevated so the guests' views are not hindered by large centerpieces.) I really like the idea of filling jars with, well, almost anything. January is a perfect time to pull out the pinecones to fill jars or vases. You may also choose to spray them with white paint or cover them in glitter. If you decide to add some color, winterberry is one of my favorite things this time of year. Cranberries sprinkled amongst oranges or green apples are beautiful, too.

For china, bring out the mismatched whites, silvers, and grays. We're creating a winter wonderland, after all. Match the patterns at one place setting while making each place setting different. In other words, if you have a silver-accented pattern at one place setting, then put white plates at the next, and off-white patterns at another, and so on. You will need a dinner plate, salad plate, and soup bowl for each setting plus a napkin in either white or off-white. Don't forget the place card. Place cards are like an accessory, the earrings to that perfect dress. They can be any color to carry the theme of the evening and one can adorn them with a simple jewel to add sparkle.

God said: This month shall be the beginning of months for you; it is to be the first month of the year to you (Exodus 12:12). Have you written down some New Year's resolutions yet? Well, I have one for you... host a farm to table experience for your friends. I promise it will be the easiest and most fulfilling resolution on your list.

Cauliflower Soup

1 head cauliflower
2 tablespoons olive oil
1 medium white onion, peeled and diced
5 cloves garlic, peeled and minced
4 cups vegetable stock
2 sprigs fresh thyme
Sea salt and freshly cracked black pepper
2 cups whole milk, optional
Grated Parmesan cheese to taste, optional

Remove and discard outer leaves of cauliflower. Slice it down the middle into quarters and separate into 4 sections. Separate core from florets. Roughly chop florets, and thinly slice core. Set aside. (If you'd like to garnish the soup with a bit of raw cauliflower, set aside 1 cup florets.)

Heat oil in a large stockpot over medium-high heat. Add onion and sauté 5 minutes until soft and translucent, stirring occasionally. Stir in garlic and continue to sauté 1 to 2 minutes until fragrant. Add chopped cauliflower, vegetable stock and thyme; stir to combine. Continue cooking until mixture reaches a simmer. Reduce heat to medium low, cover and simmer 20 to 25 minutes or until cauliflower is tender.

Remove thyme sprigs (may be used for garnish). Using an immersion blender, purée soup until smooth. (You may also use a traditional blender, working in batches being careful not to overfill the pitcher with hot soup.) Season soup to taste with sea salt and freshly cracked black pepper. Garnish with cauliflower florets and thyme, if desired. Serve immediately. Serves 4 to 6.

Marinated Grilled Chicken & Vegetable Kabobs

2 boneless, skinless chicken breasts, cubed
1 (16-ounce) bottle Italian dressing, divided
1 red onion, quartered
1 zucchini, sliced in 1-inch pieces

1 yellow squash, sliced in 1-inch pieces
1 (10-ounce) package baby
  bella mushrooms
2 red bell peppers, sliced in 1-inch pieces

Preferably the night before, place chicken in a zip-close bag and cover with Italian dressing; seal bag. Place vegetables in a separate bag and cover with remaining dressing; seal bag. Marinate in refrigerator overnight (or at least 2 hours). Next day, remove chicken and vegetables from marinade and toss on the grill (or in grill pan), cooking chicken 5 minutes per side or until meat reaches 165°, and veggies 10 minutes total, turning once halfway through. (I like to cook the meat and veggies prior to placing on skewers. It removes any doubt that my meat is cooked through and the veggies can be placed on tinfoil to cook beautifully.) Place at least 2 of each ingredient on skewers, in no particular order. Serves 4 to 6.

Cucumber & Dill Salad with Sour Cream Vinaigrette in Bibb Lettuce Cups

4 large cucumbers	Sea salt & pepper, to taste
1 cup sour cream	1 head Bibb lettuce
1 tablespoon red wine vinegar	

Wash and peel cucumbers; quarter each lengthwise, then slice each quarter crosswise. (I like to use fresh Kirby cukes with skin on, but you may use whatever you like or is freshest.) Roughly chop dill. Set both aside. In a separate bowl whisk together sour cream, vinegar, salt and pepper. Add cucumbers and dill; toss together. Chill until ready to serve. Wash lettuce and separate each leaf. With a spoon, scoop chilled salad and place into center of lettuce leaf. Serves 4 to 6.

F2T Tip: If your Bibb lettuce is not cooperating, use several leaves to make a "nest" or simply line a bowl with leaves and place cucumber salad in the middle for one over-sized cup.

Flame-Kissed Slow Roasted
Country Spare Rib BBQ

Rub:

Palmfuls of:
Paprika
Garlic powder
Onion powder
Mustard powder
Salt & pepper

Ribs:

1 rack baby ribs
6 cloves fresh garlic

Homemade BBQ Sauce:

2 cups ketchup
½ cup honey
2 tablespoons Dijon mustard
2 tablespoons brown sugar
2 tablespoons Worcestershire sauce
1 lemon, juiced
1 tablespoon paprika
½ tablespoon garlic powder
½ tablespoon onion powder
Dash cayenne pepper
Salt and pepper to taste

Combine Rub ingredients in a large bowl. Pat ribs with dry rub then fire up the grill to medium-high heat. (I know, it's January. Crazy, right?) Sear both sides then get inside; it's cold. Place ribs, garlic and water to cover in a slow cooker. (Yes, a slow cooker. I'm not a chef; I'm a mom, a home cook, and a busy woman. Therefore it is not taboo to use a tried and true method of cooking, not to mention a less intimidating method of cooking tender, fall-off-the-bone meat.) Cook on high for 7 to 8 hours. Be careful not to over-cook or the bones will also fall apart. Combine BBQ Sauce ingredients in a saucepan and simmer about 20 minutes. Heat oven to broil. Remove ribs from slow cooker, and cover on both sides with sauce. Place on a cookie sheet and broil until sauce is bubbly. Serve on a large platter. Serves 4 to 6.

Slow-Roasted Beef Brisket BBQ

2 tablespoons olive oil

1 beef brisket flat (you may get a full brisket but you will have to trim the fat)

10 fresh garlic cloves

BBQ Sauce:

2 cups ketchup

¼ cup apple cider vinegar

2 tablespoons Dijon mustard

½ cup brown sugar

2 tablespoons Worcestershire sauce

1 tablespoon paprika

½ tablespoon garlic powder

½ tablespoon onion powder

Dash cayenne pepper

Salt and pepper to taste

Heat grill to medium high. Heat oil in a grill pan and sear brisket, browning all sides. Place seared brisket in a slow cooker. Add water to cover and garlic. Cover and cook on low 14 hours. Mix all ingredients for the BBQ Sauce in a saucepan and bring to a boil over medium-high heat. Carefully remove brisket from slow cooker–it will fall apart. Trim or pick fat and separate meat into large pieces. Place on a cookie sheet, cover in BBQ sauce and place under broiler until bubbly. Serving size depends on the size of your brisket. I usually figure 1 pound of meat per person when it comes to this melt-in-your-mouth meal. However, not to worry. If your guests are stuffed by the main course, leftovers are the best. Serves 4 to 6.

F2T Tip: Obviously this course gets placed in your slow cooker the day before your event. When it hits the 14 hour mark, you may let it go a bit longer or just turn it down to warm until ready to serve.

Homemade Coleslaw

2 cups mayonnaise
1 lemon, juiced
1 (12-ounce) can evaporated milk
Sea salt
Freshly ground pepper
1 head cabbage, shredded
1 carrot, shredded

In a bowl, whisk together mayonnaise, lemon juice, and evaporated milk. Whisk in salt and pepper to taste. Toss in cabbage and carrot until well coated. Serve chilled. This is always best after it sits in the fridge for about an hour or so. Serves 4 to 6.

Warm German Potato Salad

3 cups diced peeled potatoes
4 slices bacon
1 small onion, diced
¼ cup white vinegar
2 tablespoons water
3 tablespoons sugar
1 teaspoon salt
⅛ teaspoon ground black pepper
1 tablespoon chopped fresh parsley

Place potatoes into a pot, and fill with water to cover. Bring to a boil, and cook about 10 minutes, or until easily pierced with a fork. Drain, and set aside to cool. Place bacon in a large, deep skillet over medium high heat. Fry until browned and crisp, turning as needed. Remove from pan and set aside. Add onion to bacon grease, and cook over medium heat until browned. Add vinegar, water, sugar, salt and pepper. Bring to a boil, then add potatoes and parsley. Crumble in half the bacon. Heat through, then transfer to a serving dish. Crumble remaining bacon over the top and serve warm. Serves 4 to 6.

A Recipe for Love

Ah February... the month for love and romance. It's typically one of the busiest months for our Farm to Table Experience. It is, in general, an evening of love. Because love comes in many forms, our dinners are often an evening for lovers, families, or friends.

We celebrate holidays big in our house, even Valentine's Day. Celebrations always include food, and chocolate is a necessity for this holiday. Kaden would think something wrong if he didn't come downstairs to a heart-shaped pancake, greeting card, chocolate heart, and a stuffed animal. Ian? Let's just say he'll enjoy a really nice dinner and leave it at that... wink, wink.

In February, we always sneak away to Key West for a few days. It's a long-standing Ritter tradition. Jim and Liane are kind enough to let us ambush their vacation and we're only too happy to oblige. We refer to it as a research trip, but it's actually some much-needed bonding time.

We start each day with a fabulous cup of coffee at the little French bistro that serves the best coffee in the world (really!), followed by their Americanos breakfast—a warm croissant topped with scrambled eggs and scallions with the most amazing mustard sauce on the side. We sit under a canopy of trees with, you guessed it, lights strung across from branch to branch, although our original inspiration for magical lights in trees came from our very first dinner together in Key West at Kelly's Restaurant.

We generally walk off our breakfast through the beautiful streets for miles. By the afternoon, we make our way down to where the ships dock by day. As evening approaches, the boats move away just in time for the majestic Key West sunset. This is the spot for the best Bloody Mary and shrimp cocktail in town. An evening in Key West wouldn't be complete without a fabulous dinner and a drag show (a shout out to our friends at Aqua Lounge, our best spot for research). These performers are some of the best on the planet, hands down. Best lip-syncin' ever next to Emma Stone on Jimmy Fallon busting out a rap. I'm trying to squeeze a week's worth of Key West into one paragraph. Let's just say, French coffee, long walks, the ships, the Tropic cinema, drag shows, and tattoos. We'll leave it at that.

Room Decorations

Back on the farm, this is the month I love to integrate pinks and reds into our farm to table space. It's still ridiculously cold here, so the winter wonderland theme we created last month can stay, and I like to just build upon it. We use lots and lots of layers for clothing this time of year. It's the same concept for your space. I love a soft pink to integrate in the space, not to be confused with bubble gum pink. A very subtle pink is a wonderful accent to the already magical decor without getting too "themey". Soft pink pearl garlands dripping from the tree branches are a fabulous addition to the already magical canopy over the tables adorned with white pearls, silver, and crystals. It's very subtle but makes a huge statement, trust me.

I love, love, (did I mention I love) pinks and reds together. A nice deep crimson red with a very subtle pink is a lovely way to bring Valentine's Day to the space in a very simple elegant way. Let's start at the center and work our way out. I recommend crystal, glass and silver candlesticks. I find that white candlesticks look too "candycane like" and not very elegant for Valentine's Day. I love red glass for our tea light candles as a nice, deep-red glass looks so beautiful with the glow of candlelight amongst the red and pink taper candles. This is a great month to pull out the burlap runners (however be sure to use non-drip candles otherwise it ends up looking like a bloody Halloween party at the end of the night). For me, long-stem roses everywhere are a little too cliché. Instead I love to sprinkle rose petals down the center of the table. The centerpieces are another opportunity to add a touch of color. McIntosh apples with a hint of green with cranberries poured down over them is

such a lovely addition to a Valentine's Day tablescape. Next, you guessed it, break out the rose-colored china. Neutrals, florals as well as rose all work great. The idea is to mix and match. This is the fun part folks. I do my white napkins with a burlap colored place card and a small red gemstone accent for that little sparkle.

The rest of the room needs to be more of the same—pinks, reds, and sparkle. Step back, look at what you've created. Now THAT'S romance.

God said: You shall love your neighbor as yourself (Mark 12:31). This month is all about love, so invite your loved ones, family, and friends to celebrate this Hallmark holiday authentically but also to remind us to celebrate this concept of gathering with food and love all year. Do you, perhaps, have an actual neighbor that needs to get out of the house? What better way to brighten someone's day but to have them to your home to dinner, a concept that's unfortunately been lost through the years and generations.

Hearty Baked Potato Soup

3 large russet potatoes, washed and skins pierced with a fork
¼ cup butter
1 small Vidalia onion, chopped
2 garlic cloves, minced
¼ cup flour
1 cup heavy cream
2 cups roasted vegetable stock
2 teaspoons sea salt
Shredded cheese, crumbled bacon, chives or scallions as toppings, optional

Microwave potatoes 8 to 9 minutes, or until baked through. Set aside to cool slightly. Melt butter in a soup pot over medium-high heat; add onion. Cook 6 to 7 minutes, until softened. Add minced garlic and cook 30 seconds, until fragrant. Add flour and stir several minutes to make a thickened roux. Gradually stir in heavy cream and broth. Scoop pulp from 1 potato, mash it slightly and add to soup. Bring to a boil over medium heat. Dice remaining potatoes, skins on. Add to soup and heat through. Add sea salt to taste. Soup is delicious served as is or you may top with cheese, bacon, chives and/or scallions. Serves 4 to 6.

Deviled Free-Range Eggs with Crispy Prosciutto

8 slices prosciutto
1 dozen eggs, hard-boiled, peeled and halved
1 cup mayonnaise
1 tablespoon Dijon mustard
Coarse sea salt to taste
1 bunch chives, finely chopped (or scallions)

Place prosciutto on a baking sheet and place in a 400° oven until browned and slightly crispy. Remove and let cool. Remove yolk from eggs and place in a zip-close bag; add mayonnaise and mustard. Seal bag, and mix ingredients by kneading bag with hands until creamy and well blended. Place egg halves on a serving platter. Cut a small hole in the corner of bag and pipe filling into each egg. Tightly roll up each prosciutto slice and cut into thirds. Top each egg with sea salt, a prosciutto roll and chives. Serves 4 to 6.

Caesar Salad with Homemade Croutons & Fresh Local Parmesan

Croutons:

8 slices Texas toast (or thick white bread)
2 tablespoons olive oil
Sea salt and pepper to taste

Dressing:

2 small garlic cloves, minced
1 teaspoon anchovy paste
1 lemon (for 2 tablespoons freshly squeezed lemon juice)
1 teaspoon Dijon mustard
1 teaspoon Worcestershire sauce
1 cup mayonnaise
½ cup freshly grated Parmigiano-Reggiano cheese
¼ teaspoon sea salt
¼ teaspoon freshly ground black pepper

Salad:

2 heads romaine lettuce, outer leaves removed, inner leaves torn into bite-size pieces
Shaved Parmesan cheese for garnish

Stack bread and cut into bit-sized squares. Place in a bowl and top with olive oil, salt and pepper, tossing bread to coat evenly. Place in a single layer on a baking sheet and bake at 400° about 15 minutes or until golden brown. Set aside. Whisk all Dressing ingredients together until well blended. Place lettuce in a 2-gallon zip-close bag; add dressing being careful not to over-dress. Shake until lettuce is evenly coated. Pour into bowl and garnish with croutons and shaved Parmesan. Serves 4 to 6.

Lemon-Braised Stuffed Chicken Breast with Spinach & Feta Cheese

4 boneless skinless chicken breasts
4 tablespoons butter
1 lemon, juiced and zested
1 pound fresh spinach
2 cups feta cheese
2 cups chicken broth

Trim chicken breasts and cut a pocket in each for stuffing. In a pan, melt butter over medium heat; add lemon juice. Sear chicken breasts on both sides; set pan and chicken aside. In a bowl, tear up spinach; mix together with feta cheese. Stuff each chicken breast with spinach mixture and place in a baking dish. Cover and bake at 375° approximately 30 minutes or until chicken reaches 165° in the center. Place same pan used for searing chicken over medium-high heat. Add chicken broth to deglaze pan and reduce until thickened. Add zest of lemon. Pour over chicken breasts prior to serving. Serves 4 to 6.

Creamy Risotto with Lemon Zest & Fresh Thyme

2 tablespoons olive oil
1 medium Vidalia onion, finely chopped
1½ cups Arborio rice
5 cups vegetable stock
4 tablespoons butter
1 lemon, zested
2 sprigs fresh thyme

In a saucepan over medium heat, add oil and cook onion until translucent. Add rice and stir. Add just enough stock to cover rice; simmer, stirring constantly. As rice absorbs stock, add remaining stock a little at a time, stirring constantly, until rice is cooked (16 to 20 minutes). Stir in lemon zest and butter; garnish with thyme. Serves 4 to 6.

Everyone's Irish Tonight

In March, I love to go super traditional...all Irish. Aren't we all Irish on St. Patrick's Day? We come from an area that has one of the largest St. Patrick's Day parades in the country. Whether you take your children for a family day at the parade, plan an all-day pub crawl with your college friends starting at 7 a.m. (yes, 7 a.m.), or get a sitter for the kiddos and head out with a group of friends for a Guinness or one of the hundreds of specialty beers at Cooper's Seafood House, Scranton is the place to be on parade day.

Here at the farmhouse on St. Patrick's Day, we usually wake up to the aftermath of the attack of mischievous leprechauns. They like to open all of our cabinets, turn our chairs upside down, leave their green footprints all over our floor and, uh, em, even turn our toilet bowl green.

Room Decorations

Now that we're officially inspired, let's talk about the space. I'm going to make a blanket statement by saying leave everything that's neutral, sparkles, and makes you feel happy in the space for every month. Having said that, I would suggest removing the pinks and reds for this particular dinner party. We'll go all out cliché green for St. Patty's Day, and we don't want to clash. The pearls, sequins, whites, silvers, will always be the base decor for our room and as the famous Megan Trainor says, "It's all about that base." You'll find that to be true throughout the cookbook. The song also makes for a rockin' lip sync battle.

As we work our way down from the ceiling, I would remove anything that is directly winter related. For instance, I take down my beautiful glass snowflakes and giant white glittery snowballs for our March dinner. Though I personally like to keep it simple, if you want to go all Mardi Gras on the space with colorful beads, go for it. This month typically turns into a party not just a dinner party.

Tablescape

So now that we've got the ceiling worked out, let's talk tablescape. Again, burlap runners are absolutely optional. Pros: they look super shabby chic against the elegance of the room. Cons: they're a pain in the neck to clean. You can keep several on hand and if they get too messy, throw them out.

I like to use any and all candlesticks. Bring them all out for the party. Go big or go home as we like to say in the Ritter's biz. Now, as for the candles, I really like to keep with whites, off-whites, and creams for this dinner.

I personally like to bring color with tea lights and centerpieces so break out those beautiful clear glass vases. Tip: you may use a big glass or crystal bowl or even a glass pitcher. You can do any and all shades of green tea lights in clear glass. Even orange candles work beautifully. This is the perfect month for oranges and limes. They look great placed whole in vases or halved with the vase filled with water. Honestly, if I had to choose I prefer the latter. It looks fresh and beautiful. In the market, we don't like to waste, so tonight's centerpiece is tomorrow's healthy snack. You guessed it, green patterns are our choice for china. If you do not have green available, whites and off-whites are just fine.

There are NO RULES. Be creative and have fun; the process is just as much fun as the party. I suggest white napkins for this dinner—or something neutral—otherwise the table gets really busy and less elegant. Place cards are once again burlap in color with a lovely green or orange gemstone for another touch of the Irish. In the rest of the room, feel free to use a little more green. I like a nice group of green pillar candles on my mantle. If you are using the glass lamps, fill them with limes or green apples and you can never go wrong with more candles. Remember, your guests will typically let loose at this dinner party, so have plenty of beer and coffee on hand. Get ready to queue up the dance music after dessert. Enjoy your March dinner party, you've certainly earned it. Erin go bragh.

God said: In that day, a vineyard of wine, sing of it. (Isaiah 27:2). We love the idea of wine tasting and pairings with our dinners at our winery as it offers guests an experience from the minute they walk in the door. You may not have a winery at your disposal, but the idea of pairing food with the perfect wine goes hand in hand with any dinner party. Of course, this month, Guinness is my favorite complement to our Irish-themed dinner.

Beer and Onion Soup with Irish Cheddar Crouton

3 tablespoons extra virgin olive oil, divided

2 medium onions, thinly sliced

2 tablespoons butter

½ teaspoon sugar

1 teaspoon sea salt plus more to taste

5 garlic cloves, minced

½ cup sherry wine vinegar

1½ cups medium-dark beer

6 cups beef stock

1 tablespoon chopped fresh thyme leaves

2 bay leaves

2 tablespoons soy sauce

6 slices country bread, ½-inch thick

½ pound Irish Cheddar cheese, sliced thin

In a large pot, heat 2 tablespoons olive oil over medium heat. Add onions and toss to coat. Cook 15 minutes. To caramelize onions, increase heat to medium high. Add remaining olive oil and butter. Cook until onions are brown, about 15 more minutes. Sprinkle with ½ teaspoon sugar (to help with the caramelization) and 1 teaspoon sea salt. Continue to cook until onions are well browned, about 10 to 15 more minutes. (Do not rush this process. It is the base for this savory soup.) Add minced garlic and cook for a minute more to release aroma. Deglaze pot by adding sherry vinegar, scraping up all the browned bits from bottom of the pot. Add beer and reduce by half. Add beef stock, thyme, bay leaves and soy sauce. Add salt to taste. Bring to a simmer and cook 20 to 30 more minutes.

Preheat broiler. Top bread slices with Cheddar and broil until cheese melts and starts to brown slightly. Transfer soup to tureens or individual bowls. Serve piping hot topped with Cheddar bread. Serves 4 to 6.

Boxty Topped with Crème Fraîche & Smoked Salmon

2 pounds russet or Yukon gold potatoes, peeled, divided
Kosher salt and freshly ground black pepper
⅓ cup all-purpose flour
½ teaspoon baking powder
½ cup whole milk
1 large egg
¼ cup half-and-half
4 to 5 tablespoons unsalted Irish butter, divided
Canola oil, for cooking
½ cup Crème Fraîche (or sour cream)
8 ounces smoked salmon, thinly sliced
¼ cup chopped fresh chives for garnish

Preheat oven to 200°. Place a cooling rack on a baking sheet. Set aside. Cut half the potatoes into slices; place in a medium saucepan. Add ½ tablespoon salt and cover with water. Bring to a boil over high heat. Reduce heat to low and simmer, uncovered, until potatoes are fork-tender, about 10 minutes. While sliced potatoes are cooking, grate remaining potatoes using a food processor or the large holes of a box grater. Transfer to wire strainer set over bowl. Toss with ¼ teaspoon salt and squeeze by handfuls. Wrap potatoes in doubled paper towels and squeeze to remove as much liquid as possible. Whisk together flour, baking powder, 1 teaspoon salt and 1/8 teaspoon pepper in a large bowl. Add milk and egg; whisk until smooth. Set aside. Drain boiled potatoes and return to pan. Add half-and-half and 3 tablespoons butter; mash until potatoes are smooth. Give grated potatoes 1 final squeeze and then stir them into mashed potatoes. Stir potatoes into flour-milk mixture. Heat a 12-inch nonstick skillet over medium heat. Add 1 tablespoon canola oil and 1 tablespoon butter; heat until they begin to shimmer. Working in batches, drop scant ¼ cups batter into skillet and spread into 1/4-inch-thick rounds. Cook until Boxty bottoms are golden brown, 4 to 5 minutes. Flip and cook other side until golden brown, about 3 minutes longer. Transfer to paper towel-lined plate to drain and then to prepared baking sheet. Keep warm in oven while you repeat with more oil, butter and batter. Serve Boxty warm, topped with a dollop of crème fraîche and slices of smoked salmon. Garnish with chopped chives. Serves 4 to 6.

Irish Pub Salad

½ cup mayonnaise (regular or low-fat)

2 tablespoons malt vinegar (or white wine vinegar)

2 teaspoons chopped fresh tarragon (or ¾ teaspoon dried)

1 teaspoon whole-grain Dijon mustard

2 to 3 teaspoons water

Sea salt and black pepper

4 cups torn Boston or Bibb lettuce

4 cups salad bar ingredients (such as pickled beets, sliced cucumber, diced
   tomatoes, chopped celery, shredded cabbage, sliced onions, etc.)

2 eggs, hard-boiled, peeled and sliced

4 ounces Cheddar and/or blue cheese, cut into wedges

Combine mayonnaise, vinegar, tarragon and mustard in a small bowl; whisk to blend. Whisk in enough water, a teaspoon at a time, to make dressing thin enough to pour. Season dressing to taste with salt and pepper. Arrange lettuce on a platter as base of salad. Place salad bar ingredients over lettuce in an attractive pattern. Top with sliced eggs. Drizzle dressing over salad. Place cheese wedges at ends of platter and serve. Serves 4 to 6.

Braised Corned Beef Brisket & Cabbage

1 corned beef
1 head cabbage, quartered
6 garlic cloves
1 teaspoon whole cloves
2 bay leaves
Malt vinegar

Brown corned beef on all sides and place in slow cooker. Add cabbage, garlic and water to cover. Wrap cloves and bay leaves in cheesecloth tied with cooking string. (If a seasoning packet comes with your corned beef, use that instead.) Cook on low 12 hours or longer. Place on a serving platter and let rest about 5 minutes before carving into thick slices. Serve cabbage on the same platter or on the side. Pour a little of the extra broth over both the brisket and cabbage for added moisture. Serve with malt vinegar on the side. Serves 4 to 6.

Irish Champ

2 pounds potatoes, peeled and halved
1 cup milk
1 bunch green onions, thinly sliced
½ teaspoon salt, or to taste
¼ cup butter
1 pinch freshly ground black pepper or to taste

Place potatoes in a large pot and fill with water to cover. Bring to a boil, and cook until tender, about 20 minutes. Drain well. Return to very low heat and allow potatoes to dry out a few minutes. (It helps if you place a clean dish towel over potatoes to absorb any remaining moisture.) Meanwhile, heat milk and green onions gently in a saucepan until warm. Mash potatoes, salt and butter together until smooth. Stir in milk and green onions until evenly mixed. Season with black pepper. Serve piping hot in bowls with extra butter for individuals to add to their servings. Serves 4 to 6.

Sautéed Kale with Irish Bacon

6 rashers Irish bacon, chopped (or use a thick-cut bacon with more meat than fat,
    preferably from your butcher)
2 tablespoons Irish butter
2 small spring onions, chopped
2 garlic cloves, chopped
1½ pounds kale, tough stems removed, leaves rinsed well and left damp, coarsely chopped
½ cup chicken stock
¼ cup heavy cream
1 teaspoon fresh lemon juice
Salt and freshly ground black pepper

In a large sauté pan, cook bacon over medium-high heat until crisp. Remove with a slotted spoon and drain on paper towels. Drain all but 2 tablespoons fat from pan. Return pan to medium high heat. Add butter to melt. Add onions and garlic, and cook, stirring, until soft, 3 minutes. Add kale and stir to combine. Add stock and stir. Cover, reduce heat to medium low, and cook, stirring occasionally, until kale is tender, about 5 minutes. Uncover and add cream and lemon juice. Increase heat to medium high. Cook, stirring occasionally, until most of the liquid has evaporated and kale is very tender. Add bacon and adjust seasoning, to taste. Serve hot. Serves 4 to 6.

Lip-Syncin' in the Rain

You probably have a pretty good idea of our dinner party style by now. This month is all about April showers, pastels, and spring. Here on our Northeastern Pennsylvania farm, it's planting season. Ritter's corn is our #1 claim to fame. People travel from all over to get their hands on it. We have a very special way of planting that allows our corn to be ready by the 4th of July and it's amazing. It paves the way for our famous corn chowder and corn salad.

This month, Ian, Jim Ritter, and the boys spend a lot of time in the fields getting the seed in the ground. The markets open back up full time at the end of the month, so everyone is busy preparing the markets for our customers.

Room Decorations

Here at the farmhouse, the peepers are making their debut with songs of the season out at the pond. Inside, we prepare for the Easter bunny. It's a busy month for sure. It's all about EB (Easter bunny to be specific) in this house. We decorate everything making it a really great time to be creative. Kaden and I make these very cool paper Easter eggs which can double as a centerpiece and it's also a really fun project for the kiddos.

We also have fun coloring eggs and getting Kaden's basket ready in hopes that EB loads it up with lots of candy. Mommy likes this part a lot because I often casually walk by and grab a piece or two... shhhhh! We continue our holiday celebration with a big family dinner of beef brisket, mashed potatoes and roasted root veggies and end our evening with a glow-in-the-dark Easter egg hunt which is our inspiration for the tablescape this month.

Having said that, it's time to adorn our entertaining space with umbrellas and color so we may need to do a little shopping. Starting at the top we'll hang some umbrellas amongst the trees. I recommend small, clear umbrellas so they almost look like a fun take on a chandelier that allows your little white lights to shine through them. Ensure it's the kind with a hook handle to make it simple to hang them from the branches. As usual, the more the merrier and if you have high ceilings they work beautifully. Simple, elegant, and "themey" but not tacky.

Tablescape

Burlap runners make a nice contrast to our chic look. Let's keep all candlesticks on deck with white, off-white and cream candles. Same idea for the tea lights, white in clear glass. Let's have a little fun with our glass bowls and/or vases. You'll need some plastic Easter eggs. I prefer the glitter eggs because, well, it's no secret that I absolutely love glitter, and battery-operated tea light candles. Simply open an egg, put the lit candle inside, close it and enjoy the glow. I prefer to group like colors; for instance, yellows & greens, different shades of blues and turquoise, and purples with robin's egg blue are all quite lovely color combinations. However, this is an opportunity to be creative, so the sky is the limit.

The next part of our tablescape also involves the same kind of eggs. Simply break them in half, place the same battery-operated tea lights underneath and place as many down the table as you like. The table will be quite literally glowing with beautiful spring colors and sparkling with glitter.

As for your china, anything and everything goes so have some fun with it. Pastels are perfect for this dinner so that would be my recommendation. However, think of it like the Easter eggs we color, and you simply can't get it wrong. We're coming out of winter, so your guests will be mesmerized by as much color as you can put on the table. Grouping the eggs keeps it controlled but still colorful. I like to keep my napkins white as well as the place cards and go with any pastel color gemstone for some sparkle.

I know what you're thinking. No Easter flowers? How can you have a dinner party that will stimulate all the senses with no Easter flowers? This is where the rest of the space gets a chance to shine. Flowers, as well as glowing Easter eggs, look very elegant on the mantle or buffet table. I personally would recommend keeping it monochromatic. So if you're going pink, do pinks. If you like yellow, do yellows. If you prefer to keep it super simple, then go with white. Whatever you choose will be beautiful. You cannot go wrong with Easter flowers. Although, I personally stay away from lilies as I think the pollen is messy and they smell like a funeral home. But may just be me.

Well, as we start to plant this month, there is excitement in my kitchen knowing the freshest fruits and veggies from our field are only a few weeks away. We will use anything and everything in our farm to table menus. Remember, we are cooking with color and 'tis the season.

God said: Behold, I have given you every plant yielding seed that is on the surface of all the earth, and every tree which has fruit yielding seed; it shall be food for you; and to every beast of the earth and to every bird of the sky and to every thing that moves on the earth which has life, I have given every green plant for food; and it was so (Genesis 1:29-30).

Creamy White Bean and Escarole Soup

1 tablespoon vegetable oil
1 onion, chopped
1 celery stalk, chopped
1 garlic clove, minced
2 (16-ounce) cans white kidney beans, rinsed and drained
2 cups roasted vegetable broth
¼ teaspoon ground black pepper
⅛ teaspoon dried thyme
2 cups water
1 bunch fresh escarole, rinsed and thinly sliced
1 tablespoon lemon juice
Parmesan cheese

In a large saucepan, heat oil. Cook onion and celery 5 to 8 minutes, or until tender. Add garlic and cook 30 seconds, stirring continuously. Stir in beans, broth, pepper, thyme and water. Bring to a boil, reduce heat and simmer 15 minutes. With slotted spoon, remove 2 cups bean and vegetable mixture from soup and set aside. In blender at low speed, blend remaining soup in small batches until smooth. (It helps to remove the center piece of the blender lid to allow steam to escape.) Once blended, pour soup back into pan and stir in reserved beans. Bring to a boil, stirring occasionally. Stir in escarole and cook 1 minute or until wilted. Stir in lemon juice and remove from heat. Serve with freshly grated Parmesan cheese on top. Serves 4 to 6.

Grandma Piccolo's Eggplant Bruschetta with Fresh Mozzarella Cheese and Balsamic Glaze

2 medium eggplants
Coarse sea salt
4 fresh tomatoes, diced
1 garlic clove, minced
1 bunch sweet basil, chopped
1 tablespoon olive oil
Olive oil (or vegetable oil) for frying
2 cups flour
4 cups Italian-flavored breadcrumbs
6 eggs, whisked
16 ounces fresh mozzarella cheese, sliced
Bottled balsamic glaze

Remove skin of eggplant and slice into ¼- to ½-inch rounds, not too thin. Place on wax paper and sprinkle with sea salt. (If we're using Grandma Piccolo's recipe exactly, place the Holy Bible on top of the slices. Seriously the Holy Bible, this is how I do it. However, this step is optional.) This will draw the moisture out of the eggplant. Meanwhile, in a bowl, combine tomatoes, garlic, basil and olive oil. Set aside. Rinse off eggplant; pat dry. Fill a pan about half way with oil for frying; place over medium heat. In separate bowls, place flour, breadcrumbs and eggs. Roll 1 eggplant slice in flour; shake off. Dip in eggs; let excess drip off. Dip in breadcrumbs. Fry in oil until crispy brown on both sides. Place on paper towels to drain. Repeat with all eggplant slices placing on paper towels to drain.

To assemble: Place fried eggplant on a platter topping each with a mozzarella slice. Place about a tablespoon of tomato mixture over cheese. Sprinkle with sea salt and drizzle with balsamic glaze. Serves 4 to 6.

Arugula Salad with Homemade Lemon Parmesan Dressing

⅓ cup freshly grated Parmesan cheese

5 tablespoons extra virgin olive oil

2 tablespoons fresh lemon juice

1 teaspoon lemon zest

Salt and pepper

4 cups packed baby arugula

1 cup halved cherry tomatoes

Blend cheese, olive oil, lemon juice and lemon zest in a food processor. Season dressing with salt and pepper to taste. Chill until ready to serve. Just before serving, combine arugula and tomatoes in a large bowl. Toss with enough dressing to coat. Serves 4 to 6.

Homemade Lasagna with Spinach and Homemade Meatballs

Mom's Homemade Spaghetti Sauce and Meatballs (page 9)
1 pound organic spinach, roughly chopped
1 (15-ounce) containter ricotta cheese
4 cups shredded mozzarella cheese, divided
1 cup grated Parmesan cheese, divided
1 large egg
Salt and pepper to taste
1 (9-ounce) box no-bake lasagna noodles

Place prepared sauce and meatballs in a pot on the stove to simmer. In a bowl combine spinach, ricotta, 2 cups mozzarella, ½ cup Parmesan, egg, salt and pepper. Set aside. Cover bottom of a 9x13-inch baking dish with sauce. Layer with noodles. (Noodles will expand, so no need to overlap.) Drop tablespoons of spinach-cheese mixture on top of noodles (about 12 total, 3 across and 4 down). Pour a thin layer of sauce on top. Slice a few meatballs and place them over sauce. Sprinkle a handful of remaining mozzarella and Parmesan over top. Repeat layers, beginning with noodles and ending with mozzarella and Parmesan, until you've reached the top of your baking dish, leaving a little room to prevent spillage. Cover with foil and bake at 375° until bubbly, about an hour. Serves 4 to 6.

F2T Tip: Prepare Mom's Homemade Spaghetti Sauce and Meatballs a day or 2 ahead and refrigerate.

Roasted Asparagus with Fresh Parmesan & Balsamic Drizzle

1 bunch fresh asparagus, bottoms trimmed
1 tablespoon olive oil
1 cup grated or shaved Parmesan cheese
½ teaspoon pepper
1 tablespoon balsamic glaze

Preheat oven to 400°. Toss asparagus in olive oil and arrange in a 9x13-inch baking dish. Sprinkle with Parmesan and pepper. Bake, uncovered, 15 to 20 minutes or until cheese is melted and asparagus is tender when pierced with a fork. Drizzle with balsamic glaze and serve warm. Serves 4 to 6.

F2T Food 'n' Flowers

Spring has finally sprung here in the Northeast. We're a bit behind almost everyone else in terms of cherry blossoms, but this is the month everything starts waking up from its long winter's nap. On the farm, both of our markets are up and running. Everything's a buzz as we welcome both seasoned and new employees back to the markets as well as customers from the city that are opening their lake houses again for the season.

At the farmhouse, well, it's baseball season. We live, breath, and sleep baseball. Kaden is ready to hit the ground swinging. Aside from cooking, artwork, gaming, and swimming, it's baseball that has his heart. Life becomes a balancing act regarding activities. I'm usually cooking myself to sleep after watching Kaden play ball on a chilly night.

One of my favorite things about spring in the country are the many shades of greens and yellows as the trees come back to life. I always say to Kaden as we drive through the countryside that I have never seen so many shades of green, there are literally hundreds. Would you like to guess my inspiration for this month's farm to table dinner? You guessed it folks, green. Who said it's not easy being green? Sorry Kermit, I have to disagree.

I absolutely love the mix of spring greens and yellows together; it's so fresh. It's like a room full of happy before you even see the food. Though our room will reflect this love of fresh spring colors, if you'd like to leave your clear umbrellas up in the trees, it's totally fine. It completely works for May as well. Most of our focus will be on the tablescape this month as we work to bring the outdoors in.

Tablescape

I suggest keeping the burlap runners on the table, they keep it rustic while providing a nice contrast to the bright colors. Think fresh and crisp when selecting your candles... Granny Smith apples, limes, and lemons... apple blossoms, pears, and daffodils. Think of hundreds of shades of green that make up the spring landscape, that's what we're shopping for this month when it comes to candles. Alternate many shades of green and even white taper candles down the center of the table. Yellow tea lights are a beautiful accent to the green tapers.

In our glass vases or crystal bowls, you may use yellow and green apples. Lemons and limes are a beautiful way to blend the colors of spring, and I really like the idea of citrus and what it implies... freshness.

Now that we've created a masterpiece in the center of the table let's get the china out. Whites, green, and yellow patterns or just any floral really will absolutely work with this tablescape. If you want to go all "May flowers" on your table, go for it. Remember to enjoy the process. For me personally, choosing the perfect china is my favorite part. It makes me feel like every month is a holiday and I absolutely love that feeling. Setting the stage for a dinner party is my Zen.

So once again let's mix and match our patterns while keeping the same pattern in our dinner plate, salad plate, and soup bowl at each place setting. After utensils and stemware are on the table, it's time for the finishing touches. Your place cards this month should certainly reflect our May flowers and springtime theme. Beautiful would be a neutral place card with a yellow or green gemstone or possibly a light yellow or green place card with the opposite color gemstone. If you have a yellow card use a green gem and for a green card, I suggest a yellow gem. White linen napkins are a perfect finish.

Room Decorations

Continue the theme of spring throughout the rest of your space. Bring in the large pillars for drama and top them with beautiful arrangement of spring flowers. Like we mentioned earlier, it's nice to please all the senses. I don't recommend scented candles as they may fight with the delicious smells of the food, but flowers are a subtle touch.

If you have potted plants leftover from Easter, utilize them or pick a couple bunches of daffodils or tulips for the mantle and buffet table. A few sprigs of forsythia, which are very plentiful this time of year, are a nice touch. Keeping the flowers off the table is my recommendation as there is always a way to incorporate the beautiful flowers of the season without setting them directly in front of your guests so they must converse around them. This also leaves space for food and the passing of platters family style without the fear of knocking over a tall vase of flowers.

Whatever you decide will be spectacular. There is no right or wrong. Surround yourself with things that you enjoy. This color scheme alone will make you look like a superstar. Now stand back, pour yourself a crisp glass of wine or a lovely cup of tea and admire what you've created. Now let's get cookin'. Guests are coming and this month's menu is one of my absolute favorites.

God said: Go then, eat your bread in happiness and drink your wine with a cheerful heart; for God has already approved your works (Ecclesiastes 9:7). Food is about celebration. Celebration of good health, family, and friends. I know the process can be stressful at times. Will it be hot enough? Does it taste okay? Don't worry. Enjoy the process. Enjoy the experience.

Carrot & Coconut Soup with Curried Shrimp

4 tablespoons olive oil, divided
1 large white onion, chopped
1¾ pounds carrots, peeled and chopped
1 tablespoon ground coriander
Salt and pepper
4 cups chicken or vegetable stock
½ pound shrimp, peeled and deveined
1 teaspoon curry powder
⅛ teaspoon cayenne
½ cup canned coconut milk, divided
1 tablespoon chopped fresh chives

In a large pot, heat 2 tablespoons olive oil over medium heat. Add onion; cook, stirring often, until softened, about 5 minutes. Add carrots and coriander; season with salt and pepper. Cook, stirring often, until carrots begin to soften, about 5 minutes. Stir in stock; bring to a boil. Reduce heat to medium; cover and cook until carrots are tender, about 15 minutes. In a skillet, heat remaining 2 tablespoons oil over medium-high heat. Add shrimp, curry powder and cayenne. Cook, turning once, until shrimp are opaque in the center, about 3 minutes; season to taste with salt and pepper. In a blender, puree soup with ¼ cup coconut milk; season to taste with salt and pepper. Divide among bowls; drizzle with remaining coconut milk. Top with shrimp and chives. Serves 4 to 6.

Crusty Baguette Slices Stuffed with Spinach, Artichoke Hearts & Roasted Red Peppers

¼ cup olive oil, divided
1 cup chopped artichoke hearts
3 cups tightly packed baby spinach
1 (12-ounce) jar roasted peppers, chopped
¼ teaspoon chili powder
2 baguettes
½ cup crumbled feta cheese
1 cup shaved Parmesan cheese

In a pan over medium heat, heat 2 tablespoons oil. Add artichokes, spinach, roasted red peppers and chili powder. Cooking, tossing frequently, until spinach is wilted, about 5 minutes. Remove to a bowl to cool. With a serrated knife, cut about 2 inches off one end of each baguette; reserve trimmed ends. Using the knife, hollow out the inside of each baguette leaving ⅛ inch of bread around the edges. Be careful to not puncture outside of bread from the inside while hollowing each baguette. Save the scooped-out bread for breadcrumbs. To the bowl with the veggies, add feta and Parmesan cheeses. Stir to combine.

Heat oven to 350°. Use a spoon to fill each baguette with filling. Use the handle of a wooden spoon to pack stuffing in tight. When done with each, invert the reserved trimmed ends into the open end of each baguette to create a seal. Tightly wrap, individually, in foil and bake 25 minutes. Remove from oven and raise temperature to 400°. Open foil and brush bagettes with remaining olive oil. Return to oven uncovered and bake until golden, 5 to 8 minutes more. Allow baguettes to cool slightly; using a serrated knife, cut 1-inch slices baguettes into 1-inch slices. If transporting baguettes to a party, slice and keep them in the form of a baguette, and wrap them back up in the same aluminum foil. These are great cold or room temperature. Feel free to slice, cool completely then re-wrap and refrigerate until serving. Serves 4 to 6.

Iceberg Wedge Salad Drizzled in Buttermilk-Blue Cheese Dressing

½ head iceberg lettuce, cored

¼ cup mayonnaise

¼ cup sour cream

¼ cup buttermilk

Dash hot sauce (I recommend Tabasco)

2 tablespoons chopped chives

1 teaspoon chopped garlic

½ lemon, juiced

Salt and freshly ground black pepper

½ cup blue cheese crumbles

¼ cup halved cherry tomatoes

½ avocado, diced

2 slices bacon, cooked crisp and crumbled

Slice lettuce into 4 to 6 wedges. In a medium-sized bowl, whisk together mayonnaise, sour cream, buttermilk, hot sauce, chives, garlic, lemon juice and salt and pepper to taste. Slowly fold in blue cheese. Arrange lettuce on a serving platter and drizzle with dressing. Garnish with tomatoes, avocado, and bacon. Serves 4 to 6.

Chicken Scaloppine in Saffron Cream

2 tablespoons butter
2 tablespoons olive oil
1 pound chicken cutlets, scaloppine-style (ask your butcher to prepare)
Sea salt and freshly ground black pepper
Flour for dredging
2 shallots, sliced
1 garlic clove, minced
½ cup white wine
1½ cups chicken broth
¼ teaspoon saffron threads
1 cup sliced fresh mushrooms, optional
½ cup capers, optional
½ cup heavy cream

Warm butter and olive oil in a large skillet over high heat. Season chicken cutlets with salt and pepper on each side. Dredge chicken in flour. Cook until golden and cooked through, about 2 to 3 minutes per side. Transfer to serving plate and tent with foil to keep warm. Turn heat to medium. Add shallots and garlic; cook until tender, about 2 minutes. Deglaze pan with white wine. Using a wooden spoon, scrape all the brown bits from bottom of pan. Cook until wine is almost evaporated. Add chicken broth and saffron; bring to a simmer and reduce 10 minutes. If desired, add mushrooms and/or capers and cook until heated through. (Either are a lovely addition to the dish.) Add cream, ¾ teaspoon sea salt and ¼ teaspoon freshly ground black pepper. Stir to combine and simmer 1 minute to blend flavors. Pour sauce over chicken. Serves 4 to 6.

Warm Vegetable Salad

1½ pound assorted red, white and purple new potatoes
¾ pounds green beans, trimmed and halved
1 (12-ounce) jar red roasted peppers
1 (12-ounce) jar artichoke hearts
1 bunch scallions, sliced
½ cup chopped fresh flat-leaf parsley
2 garlic cloves, minced
2 tablespoons chopped oregano leaves
2 tablespoons white wine vinegar
1 lemon, zested and juiced
½ cup extra virgin olive oil
1 teaspoon salt
½ teaspoon freshly ground black pepper

Bring a large pot of salted water to a boil over high heat. Add potatoes and cook until tender, 10 to 12 minutes. Remove to a cutting board, and add green beans to the pot. Cook until tender, about 3 minutes. Remove green beans to a large bowl. Slice potatoes in half while still warm and add to green beans. Remove peppers from jar and slice into wide strips; add to bowl along with artichoke hearts, scallions, parsley, and garlic. Toss to combine. In a small bowl, combine oregano, vinegar, lemon juice and zest. Whisk in olive oil. Stir in salt and pepper. Toss warm vegetables with the herb vinaigrette. Serve immediately. Serves 4 to 6.

Summertime on the Farm

Summer is one of my favorite seasons here on the farm. The growing season is in full swing. The markets are full of flowers and our farm to table space begins to encroach upon the front patio of our market. We open the doors to let fresh air inside. While May is always a little unpredictable, by June, our events will often spill over into the great outdoors. An evening on the porch before and after dinner is magical. Hanging baskets, lanterns, candles, and wispy ferns create the perfect backdrop for entertaining.

I love to set groupings of chairs outside with little coffee tables so our guests feel encouraged to take their cocktails on the patio. This may require a little more antiquing on your part unless you can find some extra chairs and tables hanging around. A nice trunk or chest works well as a table to set drinks or plates on for a short period of time.

Back at the farmhouse, our baseball season continues so it's still a balancing act between work and play. It is, however, well worth the juggle. I'm sure most parents can relate. Everything is blooming and beautiful so it's easy to bring the outdoors in this month. Inspiration is easy to come by, just open windows and breathe in the fresh air. By evening you may catch a glimpse of firefly or two... or twenty. It brings me back to my childhood when we would run around trying to catch them. Whenever I'm brought back to my childhood with a fond memory, it just reassures me of where farm to table originated in my life and how this is my life purpose. It's very motivating.

Room Decorations

Our room decor this month, as I mentioned earlier, should spill over into the outdoors, if at all possible. Whether you have a front porch, back patio, balcony, courtyard or yard in general, it's very nice to have an outdoor space, weather permitting, where your guests can sip on a cocktail or enjoy an after dinner liquor. Between sparkling stars or flashing fireflies, summertime is magical, all on its own after all.

Back inside, we're going a bit more casual by moving into the breakfast nook. With free-standing LED trees and a tall vase with branches, all dripping with the same magical elements displayed in our dining room, we have the same feel on a smaller scale. This is a great time to introduce small hanging lanterns with tea light candles, if you haven't already. I'm obsessed with lanterns and also love to place them with candles at the center of the table. You may also place them in groupings around the room and outdoors. Another summertime statement is the Edison lightbulb in this time when patio lights are everywhere. Hanging them from the branches right down the center of the table or anywhere else in the room is like bringing your patio inside. I wouldn't suggest, however, using both lanterns and Edison lights.

Tablescape

It is technically mid-summer according to Northern Europeans who celebrate St. John's Day and the summer solstice between June 19th and 25th. Therefore, that is my inspiration this month for our tablescape. We'll bring back whites, off-whites, and creams in mismatched candles and candlesticks. With the number of flowers and herbs available this month, they are just screaming to be stars of the show. So why not let them take center stage? For me, the idea of an English garden is so enchanting and majestic. I really love flowers in whites and purples maybe even with a pop of red. You can pick up flowers at any garden center in plastic pots (you know, the ones for your garden). I just place the pot directly inside glass jars or vases. You can always cover the pot with a little burlap. However, it's not necessary unless it really bothers you. I absolutely love gerbera daisies as an accent, but choose any flowers you enjoy, and plan to plant them after your party so they don't go to waste.

As for the china, I really love toile patterns, whites or blues for an English garden theme. Again, mix and match. The idea is to make it look effortless even though it's absolutely not. Don't forget to open the windows and let the fresh air in to celebrate the beginning of summer.

God said: A generous person will prosper; whoever refreshes others will be refreshed (Proverbs 11:25). Is someone struggling in your community? Possibly a new mom with little time to prepare a meal for her family or someone undergoing treatment for an illness or has lost a loved one? Consider cooking them a meal. I do this whenever possible because sometimes the thought of what's for dinner can be overwhelming to people in certain circumstances. We also like to invite people to our dinners whom we feel would benefit from the experience. It's always a great time of year to brighten someone's day.

Rhode Island Clam Chowder

8 pounds large cherrystone clams

7 cups water

6 cups clam broth (from steaming, or 4 cups clam broth plus 2 cups bottled clam juice)

3 slices thick bacon, ¼-inch dice

4 tablespoons unsalted butter

2 medium onions, ¼-inch diced

3 celery stalks, ¼-inch diced

2 bay leaves

2 pounds Yukon Gold potatoes, peeled and cut into ½-inch pieces

2 tablespoons chopped fresh Italian parsley

2 tablespoons minced fresh chives

1 teaspoon minced fresh dill

Kosher salt and freshly ground black pepper, to taste

Scrub clams and rinse them clean. Add water to a large stockpot fitted with a steamer basket or colander; bring to a boil. Add half the clams and cover. Steam until clams open, 5 to 10 minutes. (Discard any clams that don't open.) Repeat with second batch. Reserve 6 cups broth; set aside. Cool clams; remove meat from shells and dice it into ½-inch pieces. Refrigerate, covered, until ready to use. Put bacon in a 5- to 7-quart pot over medium heat. Cook, stirring occasionally, until golden brown, about 10 minutes. Pour off all but 1 tablespoon bacon fat, leaving bacon in the pot. Reduce heat to medium low. Add butter, onions, celery and bay leaves; cook, stirring occasionally, until onions are softened but not browned, 6 to 8 minutes. Add potatoes and reserved clam broth. Continue cooking over medium heat until chowder begins to simmer. (If it begins to boil, reduce heat.) Cook until the potatoes are tender, about 15 minutes. Just before serving, remove pot from heat. Stir in clams and herbs; discard bay leaves. Season to taste with salt and pepper. Serve hot. Serves 4 to 6.

F2T Tip: Steaming the clams might seem laborious, but it's actually easy and makes a briny broth. Aim to extract 6 cups broth from the clams; if not, you'll need to have some bottled clam juice on hand to round it out.

Mini Cornbread Cakes with Smoked Salmon and Sour Cream Drizzle

1 (16-ounce) box cornbread muffin mix, plus ingredients to prepare
1 (8-ounce) container sour cream
4 ounces smoked salmon
1 pint cherry tomatoes, halved
Coarse sea salt
1 bunch chives, finely chopped

Prepare muffins as instructed on box, baking them in a treated mini muffin tin; cool. Place mini muffins on a serving platter. Top with a dollop of sour cream, a piece of smoked salmon and a cherry tomato half. Sprinkle with coarse sea salt and chives for garnish. Serves 4 to 6.

Spinach & Strawberry Salad with White Vinaigrette and Toasted Pecans

2 cups pecans
½ cup brown sugar
¼ cup white vinegar
½ cup sugar
1 pound fresh spinach
1 pint fresh strawberries, sliced

In a bowl, toss together pecans and brown sugar. Bake at 400° until toasted, about 15 minutes, checking so they don't burn. Set aside. In a separate bowl, whisk together vinegar and sugar until blended. Place spinach and strawberries in a zip-close bag, add dressing and shake until well coated but not over dressed. Transfer to a serving plate, and garnish with pecans. Serves 4 to 6.

Flame-Kissed East Carolina BBQ Chicken

BBQ Sauce:

1 cup white vinegar
1 cup cider vinegar
1 tablespoon brown sugar
1 tablespoon cayenne pepper
1 tablespoon hot pepper sauce, or to taste
1 teaspoon salt
1 teaspoon ground black pepper

Combine all ingredients in a zip-close bag. Refrigerate 1 to 2 days before using.

Chicken:

4 chicken quarters
Sea salt and pepper to taste

Place chicken quarters in zip-close bag with your prepared BBQ Sauce. Let sit overnight, if possible. Heat grill and sear chicken on both sides. Place chicken in baking dish and bake at 400° until internal temperature reaches 165°, about 30 minutes. Add salt and pepper to taste. Serves 4 to 6.

Marinated Grilled Vegetable Kabobs

1 red onion, quartered
1 zucchini, sliced in 1-inch pieces
1 yellow squash, sliced in 1-inch pieces
1 pint cherry tomatoes
1 (10-ounce) package baby bella mushrooms (or white button)
2 red bell peppers, sliced in 1-inch pieces
1 (16-ounce) bottle Italian dressing

Place vegetables in a zip-close bag and marinate in Italian dressing at least an hour or overnight. Remove vegetables from marinade and grill in a pan on outdoor grill. Place at least 2 of each ingredient on skewers in no particular order and serve warm on a platter with grilled chicken. Serves 4 to 6.

A Farm to Table Fourth

Here on the farm, July is our biggest month. In the markets, it is all about Ritter's famous sweet corn. The men have been busy in the fields tending to their crops for months. It's now time to reap what they've sowed and enjoy the rewards of all their hard work. One of Jim Ritter's favorite places in the world is in the field on his tractor. Ritter's corn is hand-picked so it's extra labor intensive but extra special. There is no need to peel it back and check it in the market because every single ear is spectacular. As the farm to table gal, cooking with Ritter's sweet corn is pure heaven.

Back at the farmhouse, school's out for Kaden so he spends his days helping mommy in the kitchen or swimming and playing with friends. True story: Kaden begged me to submit his information and cooking video to The Food Network for "The Kids BBQ Challenge." After two Skype interviews with a casting agency (that I don't think I could have gotten through), Kaden cooked his favorite dish—grilled salmon with pineapple salsa and asparagus—in front of the culinary director of The Food Network. Unfortunately, he didn't make the cut, but he made it very, very far and we were incredibly proud. Who knows, he may just end up on a TV cooking show before his mommy.

As a child, I was blessed to split my time between two sets of grandparents. Here at the farm with Grandma and Grandpa Storm, it was all about cousins, hamburgers, hot dogs, watermelon (with the seeds), and fireworks. A few short miles away at Grandma and Grandpa Kenosky's, Grandma's July 4th parties were epic. We ate outside all day where Grandma cooked her famous potato pancakes so we got them crispy and hot off the griddle. We had hundreds of clams—I mean hundreds—and Grandpa Kenosky's famous clam chowder which I make quite often. The highlight of the day was the most spectacular fireworks display I'd ever seen. My grandpa and dad would drive to the middle of the field in his old Ford pickup and set off the most amazing fireworks while we watched in awe from the back porch. Ah, the memories...

Room Decorations

This month's farm to table is our usual monthly shabbychic dinner party. However, if you have time, also plan your very own 4th of July bash with burgers and dogs on paper plates. There are plenty of other days during this magical month to plan another party. For our dinner party, we'll be inspired by everything our vegetable and flower gardens have to offer this time of year. The sky is the limit.

If you are looking to take your party outdoors, you may choose to carry the table to your yard under a big ole tree. I have the most beautiful apple tree in the back yard that is an amazing back drop for a dinner. I typically hang lanterns from the branches which creates the most amazing canopy over the table. Do you have beautiful flower gardens? If so, that's the best. Plop a table right in the middle. It's country living at its best. If you prefer dinner on your deck or patio, then you can still create the same magical feel with large branches in pots and strung with little white lights. Be sure to hang Edison lights overhead. In this chapter, we'll stay in the breakfast nook and play it safe. You pretty much have your room ready so if you're having an indoor party you're ready to go with the June decorations.

Tablescape

Now that your space is ready, it's time to put the finishing touches on our tablescape, even if it's a picnic table. I like burlap for the table runner this month, because it adds something rustic to the table which is such a contrast from the sparkle of our decor.

Use all the mismatched candlesticks with a variety of white candles. If you want to be super-literal, mix in the red votives we used for February along with clear ones for our tea lights. In our jars, vases or bowls, I really like the idea of blue and red plums with maybe a few red cherries. It's summery and patriotic without being super-duper literal, not that there's anything wrong with that if you'd like to go that route with your decor.

The china can certainly be red, white, and blue mismatched patterns. It usually takes all three colors for me to have enough china to pull off a dinner for seventy or so people. When planning a smaller dinner, I simply blue and white patterned china. Now here's another thought... clear disposable plates. (My sister and cousins will never believe I said that, because I never use paper plates. However, I will make an exception for the 4th of July if you are serving both lunch and dinner for an all-day party.) Otherwise, stick with the plan, folks, and break out the china, that's why you have it. I really like to stick with white napkins this month but have some fun with the place cards. White cards with red or blue gemstones and red ink are adorable. Or you may use some fun stickers... maybe a little flag. Have some fun with this for sure. For the finishing touch, don't forget an epic performance—whatever that means for you—and fireworks. Hey, it's the 4th of July, fireworks are the ultimate sparkle.

God said: Rejoice in the Lord always; again I will say, rejoice (Phillipians 4:4). Remember to take time to celebrate this beautiful season and patriotic holiday with family and friends. We all get caught up in the day to day. Before we know it, our children are grown and we can only hope we've instilled a sense of tradition in them that will carry on generation to generation. This is our busiest season of the year, so I understand completely how difficult it is to plan, shop, cook, and entertain. However, life is about making memories, celebrating love, and passing down traditions. Take a moment to pause and enjoy what you've worked so hard to create. Your children will thank you later, I promise.

Ritter's Own Sweet Corn Chowder

8 ears corn

5 cups water

3 tablespoons unsalted butter

1 onion, finely chopped

3 thick slices applewood smoked bacon, halved lengthwise then cut into ¼-inch pieces

2 teaspoons minced fresh thyme

Salt and pepper

¼ cup all-purpose flour

¾ pound red potatoes, cut into ½ inch pieces

1 cup half-and-half

Sugar (you won't need sugar with Ritter corn)

Basil or minced chives for garnish

Husk corn and remove silk. Place husks in 5 cups water, bring to boil, then strain when cool enough to handle. (You may skip this step, but it really enhances the corn flavor.) Using a chef's knife or corn stripper, cut kernels from corn; transfer to bowl and set aside. (You should have 5 to 6 cups kernels.) Holding cobs over second bowl, use back of a butter knife to firmly scrape any remaining pulp from cobs into bowl. (You should have 2 to 2½ cups pulp.) Transfer pulp to center of a clean kitchen towel set in a medium bowl. Wrap towel tightly around pulp and squeeze tightly until dry. Discard pulp in towel and set corn juice aside. (You should have about ⅔ cup juice.)

Melt butter in a pot over medium heat; add onion, bacon, thyme, 2 teaspoons salt and 1 teaspoon pepper. Cook, stirring frequently, until onion is soft and edges begin to brown, 8 to 10 minutes. Stir in flour and cook, stirring constantly, 2 minutes. Whisking constantly, gradually add boiled and strained husk water; bring to boil. Add corn kernels and potatoes. Return to simmer; reduce heat to medium low and cook until potatoes are soft, 15 to 18 minutes.

Process 2 cups chowder in blender until smooth, 1 to 2 minutes. Return purée to chowder; add half-and-half and return to simmer. Remove pot from heat and stir in reserved corn juice. Season to taste with salt, pepper, and up to 1 tablespoon sugar. Serve, sprinkled with basil or chives. Serves 4 to 6.

Mediterranean Crostini

1 (15.5-ounce) can chickpeas, drained and rinsed
⅛ cup plus 2 tablespoons extra virgin olive oil, divided
1 tablespoon freshly squeezed lemon juice
1 small garlic clove, minced
Coarse sea salt and freshly ground pepper
8 large pitted kalamata olives, roughly chopped
2 tablespoons finely diced celery, plus celery leaves for garnish
12 (⅓-inch thick) slices baguette, toasted

In a food processor, combine chickpeas, ¼ cup oil, lemon juice and garlic. Pulse to form a smooth paste. Season with salt and pepper; set aside. In a small bowl, combine 1 tablespoon oil, olives and celery. Season with salt and pepper; set aside. Divide chickpea spread evenly among toasts and top with olive mixture. Drizzle with remaining tablespoon oil; season with pepper. Serve immediately, garnished with celery leaves. Serves 4 to 6.

Cucumber, Dill & Tomato Salad with Fresh Garlic & Sour Cream Vinaigrette Topped with Feta Cheese

8 cucumbers (I like to use Kirby cukes)
1 cup sour cream
1 tablespoon red wine vinegar
1 garlic clove, minced
Sea salt & pepper to taste
1 pint cherry tomatoes, halved
1 bunch scallions, chopped
1 bunch dill, chopped
1 cup feta cheese crumbles

Peel and cut cucumbers into round slices, about ½ inch thick, not too thin. Set aside. In a bowl, whisk together sour cream, vinegar, garlic, salt and pepper. Add cucumbers, tomatoes, scallions and dill; toss together. Top with feta cheese crumbles. Serve chilled. Serves 4 to 6.

Spinach & Mushroom Petite Tenders of Beef with Truffled Wine Sauce

2½ tablespoons extra virgin olive oil, divided

4 slices bacon, finely chopped

¾ cup finely chopped shallots

2 (8-ounce) packages mushrooms, chopped (baby bella, cremini and/or shiitake)

1 tablespoon minced garlic

3 cups unsalted beef stock, divided

1 (6-ounce) bag baby spinach, roughly chopped

4 petite beef tenders, pocketed for stuffing (ask your butcher, should be approximately size of your hand with a cut down the center but not all the way through)

Sea salt and freshly ground black pepper

1 cup red wine (something you like to drink, preferably dry)

3 sprigs thyme

¼ cup heavy cream

3 tablespoons butter

2 teaspoons truffle oil

Heat a large skillet over medium heat. Add 1 tablespoon olive oil; swirl to coat. Add bacon and cook 2 minutes, stirring occasionally. Add shallots and cook 2 minutes. Add mushrooms and cook 3 minutes. Increase heat to medium high. Add garlic; sauté 30 seconds. Stir in ½ cup beef stock; cook until liquid almost evaporates, stirring occasionally, about 8 minutes. Add spinach; cook 1 minute or until spinach wilts.

Preheat oven to 350°. Brush beef tenders with 1½ teaspoons olive oil; sprinkle with ¾ teaspoon salt and ½ teaspoon pepper. Stuff mushroom mixture into beef pocket. Brush all sides of beef evenly with remaining 1 tablespoon olive oil; sprinkle with sea salt and pepper. Place on a baking sheet, and bake 30 minutes. Increase oven temperature to 450° (do not remove beef from oven); bake until a meat thermometer inserted in thickest part of a tender registers 125°. Remove from oven; let stand 15 minutes.

Combine remaining 2½ cups beef stock, wine, and thyme; bring to a boil. Cook until reduced to 1 cup, about 25 minutes. Discard thyme sprigs. Add heavy cream to stock mixture and bring to a boil; cook 1 minute, stirring occasionally. Remove from heat and stir in ¼ teaspoon salt, ¼ teaspoon pepper, butter and truffle oil. Serve sauce with beef. Serves 4 to 6.

Caputo's Sautéed Broccoli Rabe with Pasta

1 bunch broccoli rabe

1 pound pasta (I prefer fresh cavatelli pasta brought to me directly from New York by the Caputo family, but you may also use orecchiette as shown)

4 to 6 cloves garlic, chopped

1 cup extra virgin olive oil

Sea salt

Crushed red pepper, optional

Trim about ½ inch off ends of broccoli rabe. Rinse well in cold water. Bring a large pot of water to a rolling boil, add salt to taste. Cut broccoli rabe into 3- to 4-inch lengths. Blanch 5 to 6 minutes; drain, reserving water. Chop garlic and sauté in olive oil slowly without burning garlic. Toss rabe with olive oil and garlic. Prepare pasta per package directions. Drain and mix in prepared broccoli rabe. Season to taste with salt and crushed red pepper, if desired. Serves 4 to 6.

Farm to Table Lazy Days

The idea of a lazy day on the farm is absurd. There is absolutely nothing lazy about summer around here. It's actually the complete opposite. However, I do like to take some time to enjoy this time of year because warm weather is hard to come by in this neck of the woods. Fishing, swimming, time at the lake with friends... I think it's very important to make memories. We get so wrapped up in our daily work, sometimes, we forget to stop and smell the roses, or, at Ritter's, the sweet corn. As a family, we enjoy the occasional drive-in movie this month because the nights are finally warm. After we've worked all day, it's really nice to do something outside in the evening.

This is also the time of year the local Daleville Methodist Church serves the most amazing East Carolina-style (vinegar based) barbecue chicken dinner, it's not too messy but is incredibly

delicious. Because we're all about food in this family, we like to pick it up and head to the drive-in for a picnic in the grass. It's a becoming a new family tradition. The Daleville Methodist Church barbecue has been a family tradition for me, of course, my whole life. You just didn't miss it. There are barbecue pits built at the church that are used one time of year only. Fine Christian women and men cook barbecue, baked beans, sweet corn, and homemade pies. It's the best.

At the farm we're plugging away, working hard, picking corn and every other vegetable known to man. Ian and his Dad are in the corn fields until sunset and Ian's Mom's in the bakery. She makes the most amazing pies you've ever tasted.

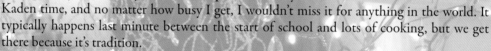

Walking into our markets this time of year is absolutely inspiring. Everything is piled high and spilling over. Fruits and vegetable are in abundance. Ian is so hands-on that most customers come in and request his help in picking out the perfect watermelon. Jim Ritter equally enjoys assisting customers with the sweet corn. This time of year, especially, is an experience from our farm to your table.

Kaden and I sneak off this month, for our traditional vacation to Cape May, New Jersey. This is our special mommy and Kaden time, and no matter how busy I get, I wouldn't miss it for anything in the world. It typically happens last minute between the start of school and lots of cooking, but we get there because it's tradition.

We hop in the car, sing songs, and head down to the lovely, Victorian-inspired Periwinkle Inn where we swim, play shuffleboard and just chill. Kaden and I like to head to the beach by day and Harry's Restaurant at night where he orders the most amazing "drunkin' steamers" and raw oysters that he talks about all year. In between, Kaden loves to make new friends on the beach or at the pool. After dinner we walk the beach where Kaden jumps from the lifeguard chair into the ocean for a swim. We also enjoy the arcade, playing mini golf, and catching the occasional movie on the beach. Our favorite is snuggling in the room while watching movies. When you're a kid, the hotel room is the best part, right?

Room Decorations

One might think this month would be all about beach decor in our space. However, I prefer simple summer decorations and cuisine that's a complete departure from barbecues and beaches. All those things are already in abundance in August, and I like to be a little different. Asian cuisine is one of my favorite influences. Therefore, that's my inspiration for this month's menu and decor.

Now this is where it gets tricky because you don't want it to look like a wedding or too "themey." However, having said that, I really like the idea of paper lanterns, Chinese lanterns in different shades of reds, oranges, and even hot pinks. Oranges, cherries, red plums (we will actually use these in our menu for a sauce) are perfect for your jar, vase or bowl centerpieces. Find unusual "spikey" flowers for the rest of your space, bird-of-paradise style, for the buffet table, sideboards and mantles. This Chinese-inspired concept can also work very well outdoors.

Tablescape

You can take the burlap runners off the table this month. I would stick to the silver, brass and/or gold candlesticks. Yes, gold, I said it. I don't use them often but for this occasion it just works. Every shade of red, orange, tangerine, and hot pink tapers will work for this theme including votives and tea light candles. The red glass vases are perfect as well. Be sure to purchase dripless candles otherwise the deep-colored wax will be an absolute nightmare.

The china can be mismatched everything. Have fun with it. Keep the napkins and place cards neutral with a lovely deep ruby-red gemstone on the place cards. Enjoy the lazy days my friends and try not to melt in the kitchen. We're going to have some fun with this menu.

God said: Their children will be mighty in the land; the generation of the upright will be blessed (Psalm 112:2). Because this month is about Kaden, we all know a week alone with your children can be gratifying but also trying at times. This verse always helps me to remember that I'm raising a future leader.

Creamy Tomato-Ginger Soup with Toasted Chickpeas

1 tablespoon neutral oil (i.e. coconut)

1 large white onion, diced

4 garlic cloves, minced

2 tablespoons diced fresh ginger

3 green onions (white stems diced, reserve green tops for garnish)

2 teaspoons paprika

2 (28-ounce) cans whole tomatoes

1 (15-ounce) can garbanzos

1 (13.5-ounce) can coconut milk

1 cup vegetable stock

2 bay leaves

Salt to taste

Heat a large stockpot over medium heat. Add oil and onion; cook until onion begins to soften, about 3 minutes. Add garlic, ginger and diced green onions. Cook until fragrant, 3 to 5 minutes. Stir in paprika and cook another 1 to 2 minutes. Add tomatoes and continue to cook over medium heat. Using a strainer or colander, rinse garbanzos thoroughly under cool water. Give them a shake to remove excess water and add to blender. Add coconut milk to blender; blend until smooth. Add to soup in stockpot; stir well. Add vegetable stock and bay leaves. Stir to combine and increase heat to medium high. Once soup has reached a boil, reduce heat to simmer. Cover with a lid and cook about 30 minutes. Before serving, remove bay leaves, and, working in batches, process in a blender until smooth. Salt to taste (I use ½ teaspoon). To serve, ladle soup into bowls and top with Toasted Chickpeas. Serves 4 to 6.

Toasted Chickpeas:

1 (15-ounce) can garbanzos

1 teaspoon neutral oil (e.i. coconut)*

¾ teaspoon paprika

¾ teaspoon cumin

½ teaspoon garlic powder

½ teaspoon onion powder

Salt and pepper, to taste

Cayenne pepper to taste

Preheat oven to 400°. Drain and rinse garbanzos. Dry them on a clean dishtowel. Discard any skins that come off. Place garbanzos on a baking sheet and drizzle with oil; stir to coat. Sprinkle with paprika, cumin, garlic powder and onion powder. Toss to coat evenly. Bake 30 to 35 minutes, stirring occasionally. Once garbanzos are firm, remove from oven and season with salt, pepper and cayenne to taste. Garbanzos will continue to firm up as they cool. Extras may be stored in an airtight container at room temperature.

Vegetable Dumplings with Warm Plum & Cider Dipping Sauce

Warm Plum & Cider Dipping Sauce:

4 large plums, pitted and cut in ¼-inch dice

1 large garlic clove, very finely minced

2 tablespoons sugar

2 tablespoons balsamic vinegar

¼ cup Ritter's apple cider

½ teaspoon sea salt

Vegetable Dumplings:

½ cup grated carrots

½ cup minced scallions

½ cup finely chopped mushrooms

½ cup finely chopped cabbage

½ cup bean sprouts

1 garlic clove, minced

1 tablespoon minced fresh ginger

Sea salt and pepper

1 egg white

1 (12-ounce) package wonton wrappers

Combine sauce ingredients in a medium saucepan, over high heat; cook 3 minutes. Reduce heat to medium high and cook, stirring occasionally, until liquid thickens and plums have softened and broken down to the consistency of a chunky preserve, about 15 minutes. While sauce cooks, combine carrots, scallions, mushrooms, cabbage, bean sprouts, garlic and ginger in a bowl; toss. Add salt and pepper to taste. Add egg white and stir to bind. Bring a pot of salted water to a boil. Spoon vegetable filling into center of a wonton wrapper. Wet edges of wrapper with fingertips; pull sides up to form a bundle and pinch together to seal. Place on a floured surface. Repeat with remaining filling and wappers. Drop dumplings in boiling water and cook 2 to 3 minutes, until dumplings float to surface and are cooked through. Drain and serve with Warm Plum & Cider Dipping Sauce. Serves 4 to 6.

Fresh Mixed Greens Salad with Ginger Dressing

Dressing:

3 cups mayonnaise
½ cup soy sauce
¾ cup sugar
¼ teaspoons white pepper
1½ teaspoons ground ginger
1 tablespoon sesame oil

Salad:

3 cups mixed greens
½ head shredded iceberg lettuce (for a little extra crunch)
½ cup grated carrots
½ cup chopped cucumber
½ red onion, chopped

In a bowl, whisk together dressing ingredients. Add water if dressing is too thick. Place salad ingredients in a 2-gallon zip-close bag. Top with desired amount of dressing. (You do not want it to be too heavily dressed. Remember, you can always add but you can't remove.) Shake well and pour into a large serving bowl. Serves 4 to 6.

Pork Loin Stuffed with Arugula and Garlic in a Teriyaki Glaze

Stuffed Pork Loin:

- 3 tablespoons bottled teriyaki sauce
- 1 tablespoon honey
- 1 teaspoon sesame oil
- 2 cups arugula, chopped
- 3 garlic cloves, chopped
- 1 pork loin, sliced into 4 to 6 pieces and pocketed for stuffing by your butcher
- 2 tablespoons olive oil

Teriyaki Glaze:

- ½ cup soy sauce
- ¼ cup water
- 2 tablespoons sweet rice wine
- 1½ tablespoons brown sugar
- 1 tablespoon honey
- ¼ cup sugar
- 1½ teaspoons minced garlic
- 1½ teaspoons grated fresh ginger
- 1 teaspoon toasted sesame oil
- ½ tablespoons cornstarch

Preheat oven to 400°. Combine teriyaki sauce, honey, sesame oil, arugula and garlic in a bowl; toss until well coated. Stuff each pork pocket, and place in a baking dish coated with olive oil. In a bowl, combine Teriyaki Glaze ingredients and pour over pork. Cover with foil and bake until pork reaches internal temperature of 165°, approximately 30 minutes. Serves 4 to 6.

F2T Tip: Leftover pork loin may be shredded for pork dumplings the next day. Just grate a cold, cooked, stuffed pork loin right out of the fridge. In a bowl, combine pork, a handful of shredded cabbage, 1 egg white and a drizzle of sesame oil. Toss. Follow instructions for Vegetable Dumplings (page 132) and dip in leftover Warm Plum & Cider Dipping Sauce. You may also dip in teriyaki or soy sauce. YUM!

Roasted Asian Green Beans with Candied Walnuts

1 pound fresh green beans
2 cloves garlic, chopped
2 tablespoons sesame oil
2 tablespoons teriyaki sauce
2 tablespoons soy sauce

Candied Walnuts:

6 tablespoons butter, softened
1½ cups roughly chopped walnuts
2 tablespoons brown sugar
1 teaspoon sesame seeds

Toss green beans and garlic in sesame oil and place on baking sheet in a 400° oven until golden brown, about 20 minutes. Combine butter, walnuts, brown sugar and sesame seeds in a bowl. Mix with your fingers until evenly combined. Place on separate baking sheet and bake about 15 minutes in same 400° oven. (But keep an eye on it. You want it to be golden brown.) In a bowl, whisk teriyaki sauce and soy sauce to combine. Toss green beans and candied walnuts in sauce mixture until fully coated. Serve warm. Serves 4 to 6.

Spaghetti Squash with Cucumber & Scallions in Lime Cilantro Sauce

2 spaghetti squash
1 lime, juiced and zested
½ cup extra virgin olive oil
2 tablespoons white vinegar
1 cucumber, peeled and diced
½ cup chopped scallions
2 tablespoons cilantro
Sea salt and fresh ground pepper to taste

To prepare spaghetti squash, pierce with a fork in several places and microwave on high approximately 7 minutes or until soft (you may have to stop and turn over half way through cooking). Remove to cool slightly. Cut in half and remove seeds. With a fork separate flesh using a downward motion (it will look long and stringy like spaghetti). Place in a bowl and set aside. In a separate bowl, whisk lime juice and zest, olive oil and vinegar. Toss together with squash, cucumber and scallions. Garnish with cilantro. Finish with salt and pepper to taste. Serves 4 to 6.

School Days

Like it or not, September is back-to-school time which means back to strict schedules and homework for those of us with children. The reality that my little man, Kaden, is getting older hits home. It's also time to start fall baseball as, once again, life becomes a major balancing act; but I love every minute. On the farm we're still chuggin' along—on the bullet train rather than a choo-choo train. Yes, things are busy. Because Labor Day weekend is big for parties and barbecues, the market's abuzz. Many of our vacationers are heading back to the city and drop in throughout the fall to stock up on their favorite farm market treats to take home.

Jellies, jams, and fresh canned goods are some of our best sellers. Summer squash and eggplant abound so that's definitely my inspiration for this month's farm to table dinner. Fall's in the air so by the end of the month the leaves start to change color and the market becomes overrun with pumpkins, mums, and gourds. At the farmhouse things are equally busy. With Kaden back in school, we're trying to get back into a routine. I emphasize the word "trying". Our free time (ha, I can't believe I just said "free time") fills up with sounds like the crack of the bat and "keep your eye on the ball!" Yep, it's fall baseball season and one of our favorite times.

Room Decorations

This month's farm to table dinner decor is back to basics. Because everyone is busy this month—because new sports, school, traveling back to the cities from country and beach homes keep everyone a little nuts—let's keep the decor simple and relaxing. After all, with the holidays approaching, upcoming months will have reason to be super "themey." We'll go back to the bare bones of the space which is still dripping with magic, but not adorned with umbrellas, paper lanterns, lanterns, Edison lights, pink pearls or anything other than little white lights and sparkle. My mother always says "simplicity is beauty" and that's the inspiration for this dinner party.

Tablescape

The tablescape is equally simple. I like the idea of burlap runners to compliment the whites. Use all your crystal, glass, white and silver candlesticks. I also recommend white, off-white, and cream taper candles with white tea lights. Fill the centerpiece jars with apple, any and all kinds. Apples scream, or shall I say whisper (keeping it relaxing, remember), end of summer, beginning of fall.

If you would like to place jars of sunflowers around the room, be sure to include yellow apples in your centerpiece jars because they are a nice complement to each other. Also include a yellow candle or two. Although, I wouldn't use all yellow; red and green are just as spectacular. I must also tell you there is nothing more fragrant than a bin of apples to give your room the most amazing natural fragrance without having to use a scented candle. If you prefer hydrangeas over sunflowers, keep it simple with a beautiful white hydrangea and a mostly white theme. There is nothing more spectacular, in my opinion. Pair it with McIntosh apples with a hint of green in your jars; Granny Smith crisp green apples or even green pears could look quite lovely. As for the china, use it all, mismatched of course. Since the rest of the decor is fairly neutral, napkins can add a nice pop of color. Also, white place cards with a little yellow sunflower gemstone are quite lovely.

If using hydrangeas, opt for a clear, white or crystal gemstone. Prepare early to alleviate last minute stress. Pour yourself a glass of wine or an herbal tea, sit back, relax, and enjoy the experience. You are becoming a farm to table superstar.

> *God said: I can do all things though Christ who strengthens me (Philippians 4:13). Remember, this may be out of your comfort zone, I've been there, but you got this. If you're not a little uncomfortable, one may ask if you are you really pushing yourself hard enough. Or do you have a little more in you? This is how we grow. You may be a little uncomfortable but that's just fear leaving your body. Once you get through it, you'll look back and wonder why you ever doubted yourself in the first place. I worked through a little uncertainty and discomfort to become an author. Are you inspired yet? Good. Who can you inspire to chase their dream? Be someone's inspiration.*

Creamy Basil-Zucchini Soup with Tri-Colored Pepper Ribbons & Toasted Pine Nuts

1 tablespoon olive oil
1 Vidalia onion, chopped
2 pounds zucchini, ¼ inch slices
4 cups roasted vegetable stock
1 cup loosely packed, washed and stemmed basil leaves
2 tablespoons sour cream, plus more for garnish
¼ teaspoon chili powder
Sea salt
½ cup toasted pine nuts for garnish
Red, yellow and orange peppers, roasted and sliced into strips for garnish

Heat olive oil in a large saucepan over medium heat. Add onion and cook until translucent, about 5 minutes. Add zucchini and cook another 2 minutes. Add vegetable stock and basil. Reduce heat to simmer and cook 20 minutes. Working in batches, purée soup in a blender. Return to pot; add 2 tablespoons sour cream and chili powder. Season with salt to taste, and garnish with a dollop of sour cream, toasted pine nuts and pepper ribbons. Serves 4 to 6.

Fresh Garlic & Cheese Crostini with Homemade Meatballs in White Wine Sauce

Mom's Meatballs (page 9),
  quantities halved
1 cup dry white wine
4 tablespoons butter plus more for bread

2 cups chicken broth
1 baguette
3 garlic cloves, minced
1 cup grated Parmesan cheese

Prepare meatballs, making them small enough to be eaten with a mini fork or toothpick. Place meatballs 1 inch apart on a cookie sheet drizzled with olive oil; bake at 400° for 20 minutes, or until no longer pink in the middle. In a saucepan, combine wine, butter and chicken broth. Cook over medium-high heat until sauce is thickened, about 20 minutes. While sauce cooks, preheat oven to 400°. Cut bread in ½-inch-thick slices. Lightly spread with butter and sprinkle with minced garlic and Parmesan. Bake at 400° until golden brown, about 20 minutes. Serve meatballs with mini forks or toothpicks with crostini on the side. Serves 4 to 6.

Grilled Caesar Salad with Homemade Croutons & Light Caesar Dressing Drizzle

8 slices Texas toast (or thick white bread)
2 tablespoons olive oil plus more for lettuce
Sea salt and pepper to taste
1 large head romaine lettuce, outer leaves peeled away, inner leaves separated
Shaved Parmesan cheese for garnish

Dressing:

2 small garlic cloves, minced
1 teaspoon anchovy paste
2 tablespoons freshly squeezed lemon juice
1 teaspoon Dijon mustard
1 teaspoon Worcestershire sauce
¼ cup olive oil
½ cup freshly grated Parmigiano-Reggiano cheese
¼ teaspoon sea salt
¼ teaspoon freshly ground black pepper

Preheat oven to 400°. Stack bread, cut off crusts and cut into bit-size squares. Place on a baking sheet in a single layer. In a bowl, mix 2 tablespoons olive oil, salt and pepper; brush over bread. Bake 15 minutes or until golden brown. Set aside. Whisk dressing ingredients together until well blended; set aside. Lightly brush romaine leaves with olive oil. Place on a heated grill; sear each side until you see grill marks on the leaf, about 1 minute each side. Arrange leaves on a platter and drizzle dressing over top. Garnish with croutons and shaved Parmesan. Serves 4 to 6.

Eggplant Rolls Stuffed with Spinach, Local Mozzarella & Parmesan Cheeses

6 eggs
1 cup milk
4 cups panko breadcrumbs
2 large eggplant, sliced lengthwise (thin enough to roll)
Vegetable oil for frying
1½ cups marinara sauce (see Mom's Homemade Spaghetti Sauce page 9)
1 cup grated mozzarella cheese

Stuffing:

4 cups chopped spinach
1 (15-ounce) carton ricotta cheese
2 cups grated mozzarella cheese
¾ cup grated Parmesan cheese
1 egg

In a bowl, combine eggs and milk. Place breadcrumbs in a separate bowl. Dip eggplant slices in egg mixture, then breadcrumbs. Fry in hot vegetable oil (about 2 inches deep in pan). Set aside on paper towels to drain. In a bowl, combine stuffing ingredients until well blended. Heat oven to 400°. Coat bottom of a baking dish with marinara sauce. Place about 3 tablespoons stuffing mixture in center of each eggplant slice and roll up. Place in baking dish seam side down. Cover with sauce until well coated. Top with mozzarella cheese. Cover and bake until bubbly, about 20 minutes. You may serve with pasta and Italian sausage on the side or this dish may be served alone. It's a very hearty dish. Serves 4 to 6.

Roasted Cauliflower "Steaks" in Truffle Oil

1 head cauliflower
3 tablespoons truffle oil
Sea salt to taste
2 tablespoons Parmesan cheese

Preheat oven to 400°. Core side down, slice cauliflower vertically across in 1-inch-thick slices. Place on a baking sheet. Drizzle with truffle oil. Sprinkle with sea salt and Parmesan. Bake until golden brown, about 20 minutes. Serves 4 to 6.

Farm to Table Fall Fun

Ah, autumn is in the air along with all the beauty the season brings. The October air is crisp and the landscape majestic. Here on the farm and throughout Northeastern Pennsylvania, people put on their big sweaters and stylish rain boots to enjoy everything the season has to offer. For us ladies, fall is just as much about fashion as anything else. Pumpkin and apple picking is one small part of the season in the country. Hot apple cider, apple cider, donuts and hearty beef brisket sandwiches are just some of the fall flavors we offer on the farm. Our customers and friends make a day of it so they can enjoy all the farm has to offer including pumpkin painting hosted by Kaden Storm, Lyla and Ethan Ritter (our niece and nephew). They know how to pack a house full of people. There is no shortage of activities on the farm and this season is one of my favorites for food. I love to offer handheld farm to table food options for our pumpkin-pickin' guests. It's just another way for our guests to eat healthy and fresh.

At the farmhouse, I finally get to decorate for fall. The yard is full of all the magical colors of the season and each weekend the trees/ landscape get closer to peak colors which is bittersweet. I do love all the seasons. So, when the leaves fall it's time to prepare for the next spectacular holiday... it's all sweet. This is Kaden's big birthday month. We'll be busy sending invites and planning a bash fit for busy boys, usually laser tag and go-cart racing. On the actual day of Kaden's birth, our tradition is morning birthday cake and sushi for dinner. October is a fun month full of parties and trick or treats.

It's also that time of year when my sister and I have our annual Halloween decorating contest. It's unspoken, mainly because she doesn't want to make me feel bad, but we give it the good ole college try over here across the street. (Did I mention that we live on Storm Road? The farmhouse is on forty acres of land where most of my cousins also live and was named after the original creators of farm to table, Robert and Margaret Storm.) Everyone likes to vote but I will give last year to my sister because she had a very scary, but tasteful, color scheme of blood red and Halloween green which looked absolutely awesome. We had a spider theme for the second year in a row but because of our lack of creativity she won by default. It really looked like our house had been taken over by ginormous spiders, so we felt accomplished.

Tablescape

We're going a bit unconventional for fall decor... no orange. I may do orange next month, but it's very easy to get tired of orange by November, if we use it in October. Leave the room just as it is, the white and sparkle are perfect. Our tablescape will definitely benefit from the burlap this month, so use it if you've got it. Candles and candlesticks are the same as last month.... whites, off-whites, and creams. Use white tea lights for sure this month. As for the centerpiece jars, bowls or vases, fill them with small white pumpkins which are so lovely and unique. Your guests are expecting to walk into a room hosed down with orange, so this is a really nice alternate. Break out all the mismatched china for this one. Anything goes, as long as it's vintage. We'll use a neutral or white napkin, a white place card with a light blueish-green (vintage looking) gemstone.

Room Decorations

If you can find Fairytale or Cinderella pumpkins at a local farm market, get them. Make a stack of those on either side on your sideboard, buffet table or mantle. Perfectly placed white pumpkins work beautifully as well when decorating the rest of the space. If you used hydrangeas last month, use them again. If you've let them dry, they look amazing in a crystal or glass vase. Your room decorations don't have to be fussy. Keep it simple and enjoy a crisp fall evening with a warm fire inside. Your guests will feel cozy and welcomed in the beautiful space you created.

Honestly, because we're so busy with our fall festivities on the farm, we don't always host our October dinner. Instead, I like to serve my favorite warm, comfort foods every weekend at the farm while people enjoy time with their families pumpkin painting, running around in our corn field scavenger hunt, viewing the classics in our hay wagon movie theatre or watching our famous pumpkin cannon hurl a pumpkin into the sky. This chapter features four of my most popular recipes served at our market during the month of October. We do have a beautifully inspired tablescape and awesome fall décor, so choose any of the dishes as the main dish for your dinner. These recipes are very appealing to the whole family and you will enjoy making these easy recipes for a quick dinner that will warm you heart and soul.

God said: "Indeed, the LORD will give what is good, and our land will yield its produce." Indeed. It's harvest time! Enjoy every bit of God's produce this season but don't forget to take time out to enjoy quality time with family and friends at the pumpkin patch as you make memories and create traditions. Don't forget to bring a friend or someone who wouldn't otherwise get out to enjoy all this season has to offer.

Homemade Macaroni & Cheese
with Roasted Cauliflower

1 (16-ounce) box campanelle pasta
1 head cauliflower
2 tablespoons extra virgin olive oil
Salt and pepper to taste
4 cups whole milk
½ stick butter
2 cups grated sharp American cheese
1 cup grated sharp white Cheddar cheese

Preheat oven to 400°. Place pasta in salted boiling water and cook until tender, about 10 minutes. Drain well and pour into in a 9x12 ungreased baking dish. Wash cauliflower, break into bit-size pieces, toss in olive oil, and place on a baking sheet. Season with salt and pepper. Roast in oven approximately 20 minutes, or until tender and golden brown. Add cauliflower to pasta and toss so it is evenly distributed. Place pot back over low heat; add milk and butter. Cook until butter melts. Slowly add cheeses and stir until completely melted. Pour sauce over pasta and cauliflower. Mix with spoon until blended. Add salt and pepper. Cover with foil and place in preheated oven. Bake until golden bubbly, approximately 30 to 45 minutes. Serves 4 to 6.

Homemade Chili

1 tablespoon olive oil
½ onion, chopped
1 bell pepper, chopped
1 pound ground beef
1 cup ketchup
1 (15-ounce) can diced roasted tomatoes
1 (15-ounce) can northern white beans
2 tablespoons chili powder or to taste
1 teaspoons cayenne pepper or to taste
Salt and pepper to taste
½ cup grated Cheddar cheese or taco cheese blend for garnish

Coat bottom of saucepan with olive oil and place over medium heat. Add onion and bell pepper; sauté until softened. Add ground beef and brown. Add remaining ingredients, except cheese, and stir until blended. Simmer 20 to 30 minutes. (May also cook in slow cooker on low 6 to 8 hours.) Serve in bowls and garnish with cheese. Serves 4 to 6.

Sweet Sausage Sandwich with Tri-Colored Peppers & Onion

1 (1½- to 2-pound) coil sweet sausage
2 red bell peppers
2 orange bell peppers
2 green bell peppers

1 onion
1 tablespoon olive oil
Salt and pepper to taste
6 fresh Kaiser rolls

Preheat oven to 400°. Cut sausage into 6-inch pieces and arrange in a baking dish. Bake uncovered 40 minutes, or until golden brown, flipping once to brown both sides. Cut peppers and onions into wide slices. Toss in olive oil; season with salt and pepper. Place in a separate, covered baking dish and roast until tender, about 20 to 30 minutes . Do not overroast; peppers should remain colorful. Place 2 pieces sausage on each roll topped with peppers and onion. Serve immediately. Serves 4 to 6.

Slow-Roasted Pulled Pork Sandwich

1 pork butt
Sea salt and freshly ground pepper
4 fresh garlic cloves
Homemade BBQ Sauce (page 32)
1 dozen Kaiser rolls

Rub all sides of pork butt with salt and pepper; place in a slow cooker. Cover with water, and add garlic cloves. Cook on low 8 hours or on high 4 hours. Remove pork butt from slow cooker and place in a baking dish. Shred using 2 forks. Toss in BBQ Sauce until fully coated and serve on Kaiser rolls. Serves 4 to 6.

Baked Zucchini Fries

3 large zucchini
2 large eggs
¼ cup all-purpose flour
3 tablespoons plain breadcrumbs
½ teaspoon salt
½ teaspoon garlic powder
½ teaspoon chili powder
½ teaspoon paprika
½ teaspoon pepper
Cooking spray

Cut zucchini into "fries." In a bowl, whisk eggs. In another bowl, combine flour, breadcrumbs and seasonings. Dip zucchini in eggs, then roll in flour mixture. Place zucchini on a baking sheet coated with cooking spray. Bake at 425° for 18 to 22 minutes, or until golden brown, turning once. Serves 4 to 6.

Farm to Table is the Reason for this Season

November is a month for family, friends, and sharing. This is what farm to table is all about. Here at the farm, we are taking a deep breath after a very busy fall season. The pumpkins have been picked, and the market is over-flowing with bins of pumpkins, apples, and produce.

This is also one of my favorite months back at the farmhouse because I can focus on family after such a busy October. It's nice to have a little breather before the hustle and bustle of the Christmas season. Preparation for Thanksgiving dinner is one of my favorite things. I love to entertain, obviously, but having my family in one place at the Thanksgiving table is the absolute best. Not to mention the food. A turkey dinner with all the fixings is my favorite meal of all time. And the leftovers. Oh how I wish they would last for an entire month. My mother's stuffing is the best. It may be my favorite comfort food on the planet. And the calories... what calories?!

This is also the anniversary month of when farm to table was born—our very first dinner, our very first menu, our very first roomful of guests seated at one long table, and our very first performance. I reinvented myself professionally and stepped out of my comfort zone with that first dinner. I want to bring it back to that first dinner so let's keep the room same as it's been, bare bones with our sparkle. At no point do you ever remove the dripping pearls, sequins, mini lights, and sparkle. If you can find a nice string of something sparkly orange or citron, that could be a really nice addition.

Tablescape

Our theme this month is fall harvest. It's the theme of the menu, the theme of farm to table, and the theme of the invitation. As for the tablescape, burlap runners definitely. Candlesticks... any and all including brass and/or gold. For candles this month, let's use many shades of orange and maybe even harvest gold (yes, exactly like that tacky color back in the 70's but it won't look tacky, trust me, nostalgic, not tacky). Tea lights are always a necessity; use glass votives and orange candles. If you want to break it up a bit, green tea lights can be a nice compliment to orange... indicative of a pumpkin. Fill your jars, vases or bowls with mini pumpkins and gourds. Use all the china except blue and a neutral napkin. The place cards, you guessed it, burlap colored with an orange or green gemstone.

Room Decorations

The rest of the room should have lots of candles and mums. I really like to combine dark burgundy and orange mums. Group them together using two orange and one burgundy in a bunch all pushed together on either side of your buffet table, mantle or sideboard. I just love symmetry.

Here's a little side note, dinner parties can be very expensive. By the time you buy decorations, food, and drinks, it can cost a small fortune. I totally get it. I can honestly say that we have cracked into our own bank accounts many times to pull off these dinners. If money is an issue at all, especially during the holiday months, you can always keep it simple. This is not about how fancy you can be or how amazing you can cook. This is about an experience. Especially this month, farm to table is about gathering people together at one table, in a space where people check their problems at the door. They forget where they are for a few hours. It's not about impressing anyone. It's about being your most authentic self. It's about spreading love, joy, and laughter with every person you meet. Farm to table is a lifestyle.

So, here's the deal, if your white pumpkins still look presentable from last month, use them or if not, toss them. If your candles are halfway burned but still have some life in them, use them, or don't. If you don't have all the pieces of china you need to make a place setting, use what you have. If you don't want to deal with cloth napkins, use paper. If you can't swing place cards, then don't; let people sit wherever they want. If you can't swing the menu I'm suggesting on any given month, use what you have and make a feast.

All those years ago when Margaret and Robert Storm invited people to their table, be it neighbors, family or friends, there were no fancy candles, fine china, tree branches, mini lights, place cards, centerpieces or crystal. But it was a table full of love. That is what we strive to create at our table each month. It is pure, genuine, real, accepting love. That is what farm to table is all about.

God said: Those who seek the lord shall not lack any good thing (Psalm 34:10). Farm to table is all about good things. Good health, joy, laughter, friends, and companionship.

Brie & Cheddar Apple Beer Soup with Candied Pecans & Oats

2 tablespoons olive oil

1 Vidalia or sweet onion, chopped

Sea salt and pepper to taste

⅔ cup Ritter's apple cider

2 Honeycrisp apples, chopped

2 teaspoons fresh thyme

½ cup Ritter's hard cider

½ cup seasonal beer (for example, pumpkin)

2 cups vegetable broth (I use savory roasted vegetable base)

Cayenne pepper

¼ cup flour

1 cup milk

16 ounces sharp Cheddar, shredded

8 ounces brie, rind removed and cubed

Candied Pecans & Oats:

6 tablespoons butter, softened

1 cup old-fashioned oats

1½ cups pecans

2 tablespoons brown sugar

1 teaspoons pumpkin pie spice

Add olive oil to large soup pot over medium heat. Add onion and cook until translucent, about 5 minutes. Sprinkle with sea salt and pepper. Slowly add cider and cook until onions are caramelized. Add apples and thyme; cook until softened. Add hard cider, beer, broth and pinch cayenne. Cook 10 minutes. While soup cooks, prepare Candied Pecans & Oats. Preheat oven to 400°. Combine butter, oats, pecans, brown sugar and pumpkin pie spice in a bowl. Mix with your fingers until evenly combined. Place on baking sheet and bake about 15 minutes. (Keep an eye on it. You want it to be golden brown, but it's quick to burn.) Turn off heat but leave in oven with door ajar to keep warm until soup is ready. After soup has cooked 10 minutes, whisk together flour and milk in a bowl until combined. Remove soup from heat and purée until smooth. (I do this in batches using a food processor. You may use a blender, or immersion blender.) Return soup to stove and bring to a boil. Whisk in flour-milk mixture to thicken, and cook another 5 minutes. Stir in both cheeses and continue to cook until cheeses are fully melted and soup is creamy. Reduce heat to low and simmer another 5 minutes or until ready to serve. Place soup into bowls, top with warm Candied Pecan & Oats. If serving family style, place soup in a tureen with the Candied Pecan & Oats in a small bowl on the side. Serves 4 to 6.

F2T Tip: You may prep this soup days ahead and refrigerate in a zip-close bag until the day of your dinner. I like to place the soup in a slow cooker on warm in the morning so it's ready for dinner and I don't have to rush around at the last minute when I'm trying to serve courses. You may need to crank up the heat an hour or two before serving if you like it steaming hot.

Honeycrisp Apple & Butternut Squash Bruschetta

1 cup diced Honeycrisp apples
2 cups diced butternut squash
6 tablespoons olive oil, divided
1 teaspoon pumpkin pie spice
Sea salt and pepper to taste
1 cup ricotta cheese
2 fresh garlic cloves, minced
6 to 8 fresh sage leaves, chopped
8 slices crusty French bread
2 tablespoons balsamic glaze (find bottled in the vinegar section of the grocery store)

Preheat oven to 425°. In a bowl, toss together apples, squash, 2 tablespoons olive oil, pumpkin pie spice, salt and pepper. Place in a single layer on a baking sheet and roast in the oven 15 minutes. Place ricotta in the empty bowl and season with salt and pepper; set aside. In a pan, sauté garlic and sage in 2 tablespoons olive oil until soft, about 2 minutes. Toss with roasted apples and squash. Brush bread with remaining olive oil. Toast in oven until golden brown, approximately 5 minutes (but watch closely). Assemble by spreading the toasted bread slices with ricotta mixture, then topping with squash and apple mixture. Drizzle with balsamic glaze before serving. Serves 4 to 6.

F2T Tip: The components of this recipe may be prepared ahead of time. Place ricotta mixture in a zip-close bag or covered container in the fridge. I also place the entire baking sheet of apples and squash, covered, in the fridge. If you prefer your apples and squash a little crunchy (I do), then only partially cook them so that when you take them back out of the fridge to reheat in the oven, they do not get mushy or over-cooked. The balsamic glaze does not need to be refrigerated. Toast the bread just before serving. If you want to pre-toast the bread, give time for it to cool completely before placing in a zip-close bag. Otherwise, it will get soggy. Serve this as a second course following soup, or place it on a serving platter on your hors d'oeuvres table.

Fresh Mixed Greens Salad with Cranberries, Walnuts & Blue Cheese Crumbles in Homemade Honey Mustard Dressing

Dressing:

½ cup mayonnaise
2 tablespoons Dijon mustard
2 tablespoons raw honey
1 tablespoon lemon juice

Salad:

6 to 8 cups mixed greens
1 cup roughly chopped walnuts
1 cup dried cranberries
1 cup blue cheese crumbles

In a bowl, whisk together all dressing ingredients. Cover and refrigerate until ready to serve. When ready to serve, combine salad ingredients, except blue cheese, in a zip-close bag. Add desired amount of salad dressing. Shake bag to lightly coat each leaf with dressing. Pour into a serving bowl and top with blue cheese crumbles. Lightly mix to distribute blue cheese but be careful not to over mix. Serves 4 to 6.

Maple-Glazed Salmon

2 tablespoon Dijon mustard
¼ cup pure maple syrup
Salt and pepper to taste
2 tablespoons olive oil
4 to 6 skinless salmon fillets, 6- to 8-ounces each
3 sprigs fresh thyme

In a bowl, whisk together mustard and maple syrup to form a thick glaze. Add salt and pepper to taste. Add olive oil to skillet over medium-high heat. Lightly salt and pepper both sides of salmon fillets. Brush 1 side with glaze and place in heated skillet, glaze side down. Use remaining glaze mixture to brush tops of fillets. Cook salmon 2 to 3 minutes on each side to get a nice sear. If you prefer your salmon cooked a bit more, simply turn off heat and cover until desired temperature is reached. Cooking time may vary based on thickness of salmon fillets. Place on a serving platter and drizzle with remaining glaze from pan. Garnish with fresh thyme sprigs. Serves 4 to 6.

F2T Tip: If you would like a stronger maple flavor, marinate salmon fillets by placing them in a zip-close plastic bag and pouring glaze over them, reserving 2 tablespoons. Refrigerate up to 1 hour. Follow cooking instructions above and brush with remaining glaze from marinade.

Creamy Mashed Potatoes

4 to 6 large white potatoes, washed and roughly chopped
1 cup whole milk
4 tablespoons butter
Sea salt and freshly ground pepper

Place potatoes in a pot with salted water to cover. Bring to a boil and cook 15 to 20 minutes after water starts to boil or until tender when pierced with a fork. Drain well and return to pot. Add milk and butter. With hand blender, beat until creamy. Add sea salt and pepper to taste. Serves 4 to 6.

Roasted Autumn Squash

3 acorn squash
6 tablespoons butter, divided
¼ cup brown sugar, divided
Sea salt
Pumpkin pie spice
Fresh maple syrup to drizzle

Preheat oven to 400°. Cut squash in half; remove seeds and scrape out inside. Cut into quarters and place in baking dish, skin side down, with water just covering the bottom of the dish. Place ½ tablespoon butter and 1 teaspoon brown sugar in each squash quarter. Sprinkle with sea salt and pumpkin pie spice to taste. Bake 25 minutes or until center is soft when pierced with a fork. Place on serving platter and drizzle with maple syrup. Serves 4 to 6.

Roasted Brussels Sprouts in Truffle Oil and Parmesan

1 pound fresh Brussels sprouts, halved
2 tablespoons truffle oil
3 garlic cloves, minced
½ cup Parmesan cheese
⅛ teaspoon pepper
Dash sea salt

Place Brussels sprouts on a baking sheet. Combine truffle oil, garlic and Parmesan; drizzle over sprouts and toss to coat. Sprinkle with pepper and salt. Bake, uncovered, at 450° for 10 to 15 minutes or until tender and crispy, stirring occasionally. Serves 4 to 6.

Farm to Table Festive

The holiday season has begun here at the farm. Since Thanksgiving, our customers have been selecting the perfect, fresh-cut tree for their homes where the stockings are hung by their chimney with care. The markets are filled with all the sights and smells of the season. It's the most wonderful time of the year and holiday parties are all the rage this month.

Back at the farmhouse, we celebrate Christmas and also get ready for Santa Clause so there is no shortage of traditional holiday decorations. There's another big birthday this month. And if you haven't guessed, it's mine! We celebrate with a full-on family dinner usually cooked by my amazing mother.

My birthday weekend, Kaden and I hike out to the tree farm to score the biggest tree we can cut down... it's our tradition. We also get our Ritter family Christmas tree at the farm so, yes, we get two trees. In this way, I can see a Christmas tree from multiple locations in my home. And, I like one traditional tree with colorful lights that remind me of my grandma's tree, and one with white lights.

I love fresh wreaths, but sometimes that is not in the budget. My little trick? I take my real-looking "fake" wreaths that I invested in a long time ago and stick my leftover Christmas tree clippings in them. You honestly can't tell the difference.

Room Decorations

So, let's talk about our space. Remember the decorations we bought at discounted prices back in January? It's time to get them out and start creating our winter wonderland once again. I like to hang big, white, glitter snowballs and pretty, clear snowflakes in additional to everything that's already dripping from the tree branches.

Because we sell Christmas trees in the market, there is no shortage for our space. We even hang a Christmas tree or two from the ceiling. For decorations, typically I use green lights to reflect a feeling of freshness. I then use burlap for the garland. You can pick up rolls of burlap at Christmas tree shops that is used to cover shrubs, so it's very inexpensive. I use clear, green ornaments and curly glitter sticks (green and silver) to complete the look. I'm drawn to a monochromatic look, but feel free to use whatever you have or whatever makes you personally happy. Anything will work for this holiday and there are so many ornaments available this time of year if you can swing it.

When purchasing the farmhouse for my family, I planted shrubs that could be used for decorations inside the house. I clip branches from my holly trees (preferably the ones with berries) and put them in vases. I also always enjoy lots of candles around the room and stockings on the mantle, the burlap kind, of course.

If you want to pull out those red votives with tea lights for your buffet table, sideboard or mantle, it is a beautiful accent that compliments the cranberries and holly berries. I also love to decorate with old, antique doors from my house. I just stick them up against the wall, and hang a grapevine wreath with a white bow on the doors.

Tablescape

Now because we originally created this farm to table experience in November, when December came around I didn't want to change very much around the room. So, having said that, I really like the look of the burlap table runners, every candlestick you can get your hands on, and the various white candles. The look is so elegant for the holiday. For the centerpieces, I love fresh limes and cranberries in the jars, bowls, and vases. It's a subtle touch of red and green yet makes a statement. Use all the china as well for this event. I suggest white napkins with white burlap-colored place cards with a silver or gold gemstone. This is a month of great joy and celebration no matter what you believe or what you are celebrating. It is a time for family, celebration, and reflection. Enjoy the festivities, especially the one you just created.

> *God said: The angel said to them, "Do not be afraid; for behold, I bring you good news of great joy which will be for all the people." (Luke 2:10). I always remember that scene in A Charlie Brown's Christmas where Linus stands on the stage and says this line. It gives me chills every time. Amongst the hustle and bustle of the season let's remember to be grateful for our many blessings, family, friends, and good health. What better way to do it but around the table with the people we love in a room sparkling with all the magic of the season?*

Kale, Sausage and Lentil Soup

2 teaspoons extra virgin olive oil

8 ounces sweet Italian sausage, casings removed

2 celery stalks with leafy tops, thinly sliced

1 medium Vidalia onion, diced medium

½ cup dried lentils

6 cups roasted vegetable broth

1 bunch (about ½ pound) kale (preferably Tuscan), stems removed and torn into bite-size pieces

Coarse sea salt and ground pepper to taste

2 teaspoons red wine vinegar

In a large Dutch oven or heavy pot, heat oil over medium-high heat. Add sausage and cook, breaking up meat with a wooden spoon, until brown, about 5 minutes. Add celery and onion; cook until softened, about 5 minutes. Add lentils, broth and ½ cup water; bring to a boil. Reduce heat to medium low and bring soup to a rapid simmer. Partially cover and cook until lentils and vegetables are tender, 25 minutes. Add kale and season with salt. Return soup to a rapid simmer, cover, and cook until kale wilts, about 5 minutes. Remove soup from heat, stir in vinegar and season with salt and pepper. Serves 4 to 6.

Wild Mushroom Risotto Rounds

1 batch Creamy Risotto (page 53)
2 cups shiitake or baby bella mushrooms, chopped
2 tablespoons butter
2 cups flour
2 cups breadcrumbs
6 eggs
½ cup milk
Vegetable oil for frying

Prepare risotto as directed. While it cooks, sauté mushrooms in butter in a small saucepan over medium heat. Add to risotto and mix in evenly. Refrigerate until completely cool. Once cooled, form risotto into balls about the size of a meatball and place on a baking sheet covered with wax paper. Return to fridge to keep cool. Place flour and breadcrumbs into separate bowls. Whisk milk and eggs together in a third bowl. Heat oil for deep frying. Remove risotto balls and, working 1 at a time, place each in flour first; shake off. Next dip in egg mixture, let excess drip off. Then dip in breadcrumbs. Last, fry in oil until dark, crispy brown on both sides. Place on paper towels to drain. Serves 4 to 6.

Hearts of Romaine Salad with Roasted Red Peppers, Artichoke Hearts and Homemade Croutons in Italian Vinaigrette

1 loaf French bread, cubed

2 tablespoons olive oil

Sea salt and fresh ground pepper to taste

2 heads Romaine lettuce, outer leaves pulled away and chopped

1 (10-ounce) jar roasted red peppers, roughly chopped

1 (12-ounce) jar artichoke hearts, roughly chopped

1 (16-ounce) jar Ken's Italian Dressing

Preheat oven to 400°. Lighly toss bread cubes in olive oil and spread in single layer on a baking sheet. Sprinkle with salt and pepper to taste. Bake until golden brown, about 15 to 20 minutes. (Watch closely to prevent burning.) Set aside. In a zip-close bag, combine lettuce, red peppers and artichoke hearts. Add dressing to taste and shake until well coated. Pour in bowl and garnish with croutons. Serves 4 to 6.

Fresh Homemade Eggplant Parmesan

Chunky Tomato Sauce:

Vegetable oil
2 cups finely chopped onion
2 cups finely chopped celery
2 cups shredded carrots
1 tablespoon sweet basil
1 tablespoon parsley
1 tablespoon oregano
Salt and pepper
1 (28-ounce) can whole tomatoes
2 (28-ounce) cans crushed tomatoes
¾ tablespoon sugar

Coat bottom of large pot with oil. When heated, add vegetables, herbs, salt and pepper; cook until tender and translucent. Add tomatoes and sugar. Simmer 2 to 3 hours. This light sauce is perfect for Eggplant Parmesan which can be such a heavy dish. Sauce may be made ahead and used later (even cold) to assemble Eggplant Parmesan.

Eggplant:

Olive oil
2 large eggs
2 tablespoons milk
¾ cup panko breadcrumbs
¾ cup plus 2 tablespoons Parmesan cheese, divided
Coarse salt and ground pepper
2 large eggplants (2½ pounds total), peeled and sliced into ½-inch rounds
1½ cups shredded mozzarella cheese

Preheat oven to 350°. Heat oil in a pan over medium-high heat. In a bowl, whisk together eggs and milk. In another bowl, combine panko and ¾ cup Parmesan; season with salt and pepper. Dip each eggplant slice in egg mixture, letting excess drip off, then dredge in breadcrumb mixture, coating well. Place in skillet in batches (do not crowd) and cook 3 to 4 minutes each side, turning once, until golden brown. Let sit on paper towels to drain. Spread a light layer of sauce in a 9x13-inch baking dish. Arrange half the eggplant in dish; cover with 2 cups sauce, then ½ cup mozzarella. Repeat with remaining eggplant, sauce and mozzarella; sprinkle with 2 tablespoons Parmesan. Bake until sauce is bubbly and cheese is melted, 15 to 20 minutes. Let stand 5 minutes before serving. Serves 4 to 6.

Sautéed Spaghetti Squash with Fresh Herbs & Garlic

2 spaghetti squash
3 garlic cloves, minced
½ cup extra virgin olive oil
1 bunch basil, chopped
1 bunch parsley, chopped
Sea salt and fresh ground pepper to taste

Pierce one squash with a fork and microwave on high approximately 7 minutes or until soft (stop and turn over half way through cooking). Repeat with second squash and set aside to cool slightly. Cut each squash in half and remove seeds. With a fork, separate flesh using a downward motion (it will look long and stringy like spaghetti). Place in a bowl set aside. Sauté garlic in a pan with olive oil until slightly browned. Pour over spaghetti squash and toss in basil and parsley. Add salt and pepper to taste. Serves 4 to 6.

Let's Do Brunch

Field of Dreams is one of my favorite baseball movies of all time. I'd been searching for a copy all summer long and couldn't seem to find it anywhere. My father passed over the summer, and because that movie always reminds me of playing catch with him, I really felt it would help me heal. After finally finding the movie, I watched it a few nights ago. In the final scene, Ray yells, "Hey Dad, you wanna have a catch?" with childlike innocence (before a difficult life changed him and he got away from his authentic self). His father turns around and replies, "I'd like that." And then they had a catch. This is where I sit in a puddle of tears with a tub of ice cream.

Baseball was my life as a child. It was our family time. From t-ball to missy league, my dad coached most of my teams. I'll never forget my very first day of t-ball practice which ended up being cancelled because of a complete washout. I was so disappointed as I sat by our sliding glass door looking outside, praying the rain would stop. Of course, my mother cooked a fabulous meal that made me quickly forget my troubles.

My little sister and all our cousins played on the Mercuries Magic team, too. My dad coached us all the way to victory several times as my mom, aunts, and uncles sat in the stands cheering us on. After every game, we would all jump in the back of Dad's blue Mazda pick-up truck to reap our reward of ice cream after a long hard game. My biggest worry back then... do I order mint chocolate chip or black raspberry?

Baseball always brings me back to a time of pure authenticity, joy, and happiness. *Field of Dreams* is about all those things... about going back to a place where you feel that childlike innocence again. If you've never seen the movie, I highly recommend you watch it because it's exactly what farm to table is all about. It's the message I received from God very early on, "If you build it, they will come." It's how I knew I was on the right path.

I recently received a similar message... if you write it, they will come... the missing piece of the puzzle and the one thing I needed to hear to truly make farm to table an even bigger success. In addition to wonderful recipes and stories, the message I want you to take away after reading this book is the feeling of pure authenticity, joy, and happiness you will feel when you "build" a farm to table experience and "they come."

Baseball always brings me back to a time of pure authenticity.

Last night I dreamt of a road I always walked on as a child with my cousins—"skipped down" is probably the more accurate phrase. I skipped down that road every day. Back then, we didn't worry about "adulting." We were kids! We didn't worry about what was for dinner, bills, illness, what time to pick the kids up for activities, cleaning the house. You get the idea. We were open to anything and everything... living in the moment... finding joy in the little things. There were no worries about tomorrow or the future. We played, built forts out of nothing but a few twigs, and skipped as we helped Grandpa feed the chickens. In short, we were our true authentic selves... who God created us to be in His image before life began to mold us and life's events started to affect us. It's before you worry about what others think of you... that place where miracles happen... where we can still connect with God in a childlike way. It's the place where we don't over-analyze or over-think. We are willing to quiet our minds and listen to what God wants us to hear. Our life's purpose. It's okay if you didn't have the perfect childhood because God breathed life into you. Therefore, that perfect child is in you somewhere. You may have to ask God to help show it to you, but it is within you.

I am fortunate enough to live on that very road where I played as a child. Nowadays, as I walk down the road with my son or my dog, if I'm not engaged in conversation, my mind is always thinking about what I need to do after my walk. My inner dialogue sounds something like this: "what's for dinner before we have to leave for baseball", "did I remember to put the clothes in the dryer", "I better unload the dishwasher before we leave", "do I need to run to the store for anything".

Today, I tried something new. I walked down the road and decided to skip a little. I reminisced a lot. Then it occurred to me that in my dream I veered off Storm Road and walked down the little side road that I don't walk on very often. So this day, I took a different path on my way home. That was where it hit me loud and clear. I felt as though God was speaking to me directly in that moment, on that little side road.

> ...that place where creativity flows, where we effortlessly help others.

To achieve our goals, we need to get back to our most authentic selves. We need to tap into that child in all of us. It's in that place where creativity flows, where we effortlessly help others. We share, we exude happiness and are free from the worries that distract us from our soul's true purpose. It's in that place where we experience pure authentic joy and there are no limits or blocks to what we achieve. Imagine a world where we not only teach our children that it's okay to play but we as adults allow ourselves that time. Furthermore, not only do we allow the time, but we actually enjoy it. Imagine what you will create through the eyes of your inner child where everything isn't a chore, where everything isn't something you have to do but you do it because you want to do it. That's the world God wants for us. We tend forget that along the way. We drag ourselves to jobs to collect a paycheck then home to more work and exhaustion... only to do it all again the next day. If we're lucky, we have enough energy for family time and our children, sometimes.

Well, it's time for a change. It's time for us to tap into that child inside in a way that will have us all living our soul's purpose with excitement (remember that excitement?) and as a result, experiencing pure authentic joy and happiness. Creating in the kitchen brings me pure joy and I sincerely hope that you feel it too. That's what farm to table is all about—spreading a little joy through food and sharing with others around your table.

So, what do I recommend? Before you do anything, before you start, go back. Go back in your mind or take a walk where you grew up. Maybe watch a movie that brings you back or meet with an old childhood friend. When I'm around my sister or cousins, I instantly turn into a goofy little girl.

Go back! It will help you hit the reset button in your mind as well as your life. Remember who you were before someone told you who you are supposed to be. From there, the sky is the limit. You will create like a child with no blocks, nothing holding you back, no overthinking. You will leap literally and figuratively like a child. You will spread more joy and happiness than you can imagine, and people will want more. They will crave it. They will beg you to come back or ask you to show them how to achieve it. The joy will be contagious. The laughter will be free flowing. You will sing and dance as if no one is watching... cook and not care about what others think but rather how it makes them feel. You will feed their souls. If you create your experience through the eyes of a child, free of fear and worry, imagine how sensational it will be.

When I was a little girl, sleeping at my Grandma's farmhouse with my cousins was a weekly occurrence. In the summertime, we'd build forts in the woods, play kickball with the neighbors by day, and catch fireflies and play hide-and-seek at night. We'd all go to church with Grandma in the morning if we slept over on a Saturday night, and on a school night, we'd lay our clothes out in every room of the house for school the next morning. In the winter, we prayed for a snow day, so we could go sledding all day and come in for Grandma's hot chocolate and cookies.

We always went to bed with our "Now I lay me down to sleep..." prayer, and Grandma always read *Cinderella*, one of my favorite bedtime stories of all time. I feel like I can still hear her saying my favorite line "Bippity Boppity Boo"! No matter what we did during the day or in the evening, one thing was always certain. We would wake up to the smell of her warm maple syrup on the stove.

Today, although my grandparents are in Heaven watching over us (I'm certain of that), I still live in that same farmhouse. I'm fortunate that I get to cook in the same kitchen. Although it may look a little different, the feeling is still the same. Memories are made on the weekends over breakfast or a tasty dessert for a special occasion. The smell of something sweet or even warm and savory baking in the kitchen means it's a special day. In this brunch chapter, I'm including some of my favorite nostalgic breakfast dishes and desserts from my family to yours. I hope they become a part of your family's traditions, too. They're simple enough to have the kiddos help and make a fun memory for any special occasion. After all, there's always room for dessert and time for breakfast... farm to table style.

> *God said: Do all things without grumbling or disputing: so that you will prove yourselves to be blameless and innocent, children of God above reproaching the midst of a crooked and perverse generation, among whom you appear as lights in the world (Philippians 2:14-15). You are a child of God. Be the light. It is, indeed, inside of you.*

Grandma's Hot Cocoa

3½ teaspoons cocoa powder
5 teaspoons sugar
½ teaspoon salt
1 teaspoon vanilla
½ cup water
4 cups whole milk

Mix all ingredients in a saucepan and bring to a boil. Serve hot.

Classic Mimosa with Frozen Blueberries

¼ cup sugar

¼ cup water

½ cup frozen blueberries (for a seasonal twist, add frozen cranberries)

¼ cup chilled orange juice

¾ cup chilled champagne (or lemon-lime soda)

Fresh orange slice, optional

Pour sugar evenly onto a flat plate. On a separate plate pour water. Take tall champagne or wine glass, dip in water and then sugar to rim glass. Pour frozen blueberries into glass. Add orange juice and champagne; stir and serve chilled. May garnish with orange slice. Serves 1.

Summer Peach and Tomato Salad with Raspberry Vinaigrette

6 peaches (or nectarines depending on seasonal freshness)
3 medium tomatoes, halved then thinly sliced in wedges
1 pint cherry tomatoes, halved
½ red onion, thinly sliced
¼ cup raspberry vinaigrette salad dressing
½ cup walnuts, roughly chopped

In a large bowl, combine peaches, tomatoes and onion. Toss in raspberry vinaigrette until evenly coated. Top with chopped walnuts. May be served chilled or room temperature. Serves 4 to 6.

Roasted Potatoes with Fresh Garlic

6 white potatoes, cubed

4 garlic cloves, chopped

¼ teaspoon garlic powder

¼ teaspoon onion powder

¼ teaspoon paprika

¼ teaspoon dried rosemary

¼ teaspoon dried oregano

¼ cup olive oil

Sea salt and pepper to taste

Preheat oven to 400°. In a bowl, toss potatoes, garlic and herbs in olive oil until evenly coated. Arrange evenly in baking dish and season with salt and pepper. Bake 30 minutes, tossing occasionally, until golden brown and crispy. Serves 4 to 6.

Grandma's Banana Bread

1 cup sugar
2½ cups flour
3 tablespoons vegetable oil
1 cup mashed banana (preferably overripe)
1 teaspoon salt
3½ teaspoons baking powder
¾ cup milk
1 egg

Preheat oven to 350°. Combine ingredients in a bowl; mix until blended. Transfer to a greased loaf pan and bake 45 minutes to 1 hour, or until a toothpick inserted in center comes out clean.

Grandma's Zucchini Bread

2 cups grated fresh zucchini
½ cup vegetable oil
2 cups sugar
2 cups flour
3 eggs, beaten until frothy
2 teaspoons baking soda
¼ teaspoon baking powder
1 teaspoon salt
1 teaspoon cinnamon
1 teaspoon vanilla
1 cup chopped nuts, optional

Preheat oven to 350°. Combine all ingredients. Pour into 2 greased loaf pans and bake 1 hour.

Easy Blueberry Pancake Casserole with Maple Syrup Drizzle

1 (16-ounce) box pancake or waffle mix
2 pints blueberries
1 (8-ounce) bottle pure maple syrup

Preheat oven to 400°. In a bowl, prepare entire contents of mix per instructions on box. Add blueberries; stir gently until evenly combined. Pour into greased 8½x8½-inch baking dish. Bake approximately 30 minutes until golden brown. Drizzle with maple syrup and serve warm. Serves 6 to 8.

Overnight French Toast Casserole

8 eggs

1½ cups milk

1 teaspoon cinnamon

2 teaspoons pure vanilla extract

12 slices Texas Toast (approximately 1 loaf)

2 pints blueberries, optional

4 tablespoons butter

1 cup brown sugar

1 (8-ounce) bottle pure maple syrup

In a bowl, whisk together eggs, milk, cinnamon and vanilla. Tear bread into bite-size pieces and stir into egg mixture until each piece is well coated. Slowly fold in blueberries. Pour into greased 8½x8½-inch baking dish; set aside. In a small saucepan, combine butter and brown sugar; simmer until bubbly. Pour over top of bread and egg mixture in baking dish; cover with plastic wrap and place in refrigerator overnight. When ready to eat, preheat oven to 400° and bake about 30 minutes until golden and bubbly. Serve warm with maple syrup drizzle. Serves 4 to 6.

Baked Italian Frittata

1 pint cherry or grape tomatoes, halved
¼ cup olive oil
12 eggs
½ cup milk
1 bunch fresh basil
¾ cup each shredded Mozzarella, Provolone and Parmesan cheese
Salt and pepper to taste

Preheat oven to 400°. Toss tomatoes in olive oil and arrange evenly on baking sheet. Bake about 15 to 20 minutes until golden brown; set aside. In a bowl, whisk together eggs and milk. Add basil, tomatoes, cheeses, salt and pepper. Pour into greased 9x13-inch baking dish. Bake 30 minutes or until mixture resembles consistency of custard. Do not overbake. Serves 4 to 6.

Fresh Summer Squash and Zucchini Frittata

12 eggs

½ cup milk

1 small red onion, chopped

1 (4-ounce) jar julienne-cut sun-dried tomatoes in oil

1 medium zucchini, halved then cut in ¼-inch slices

1 medium yellow squash, halved then cut in ¼-inch slices

4 ounces Feta cheese, crumbled

Salt and pepper to taste

Preheat oven to 400°. In a bowl, whisk together eggs and milk. Add onion, tomatoes, zucchini, squash, Feta, salt and pepper. Pour into greased 9x13-inch baking dish. Bake 30 minutes or until mixture resembles consistency of custard. Be careful not to overbake. Serves 4 to 6.

Baked Tex-Mex Frittata

12 eggs
½ cup milk
½ Vidalia or sweet onion
1 red bell pepper, chopped
1 green bell pepper, chopped
1 orange bell pepper, chopped
1 medium tomato, chopped
1 cup shredded Cheddar cheese
1 cup shredded Monterey cheese
Salt and pepper to taste

Preheat oven to 400°. In a bowl, whisk together eggs and milk. Add onion, peppers, tomato, cheeses, salt and pepper. Pour into greased 9x13-inch baking dish. Bake 30 minutes or until mixture resembles consistency of custard. Be careful not to overbake. Serves 4 to 6.

Grandma's Crumb Cake

3 cups flour
2 cups sugar
½ cup butter, softened
2 teaspoons baking powder
Pinch salt
2 eggs
1 cup milk

Preheat oven to 350°. In a bowl, mix flour, sugar, butter, baking powder and salt until crumbly. Reserve 1 cup for topping. To remaining mixture, add eggs and milk. Place in a greased 9x12-inch baking dish (smaller for thicker cake) and sprinkle remaining crumbs on top. Bake 1 hour, or until a toothpick inserted into center comes out clean.

Mom's Homemade Rice Pudding

6 cups milk
2 cups water
1 stick butter
1 cup white rice
2 eggs
1 cup sugar
1½ teaspoons vanilla

In a saucepan, combine milk, water, butter and rice. Bring to a boil; cover and simmer 45 minutes. Remove from heat. In a separate bowl, mix eggs, sugar and vanilla. Stir into cooked rice while still hot and chill until ready to serve. Garnish with cinnamon stick or sprinkle with cinnamon prior to serving.

F2T Tip: A candy thermometer reading 165° after the egg mixture is added to the rice mixture will confirm the eggs are fully cooked.

Snickerdoodle Cookies

1½ cups sugar plus more for coating
½ cup shortening (or 1 stick butter, softened)
2 eggs
2¾ cups flour
2 teaspoons cream of tartar
1 teaspoon baking soda
¼ teaspoon salt
Cinnamon for coating

Preheat oven to 350°. In a bowl, combine ingredients, except cinnamon, until blended. Combine sugar and cinnamon to taste. Roll dough into small balls and drop in sugar-cinnamon mixture. Place on greased baking sheet 2 inches apart. Bake 10 to 12 minutes or until light golden brown.

Grandma's White Fudge

3 cups sugar
Pinch salt
1 tablespoon vanilla
⅔ cup Carnation evaporated milk
⅓ cup milk
½ stick butter
1 cup chopped nuts, optional

Combine ingredients in small pot over medium-high heat; cook to a rolling boil. Continue to cook, stirring constantly until it thickens slightly. Place candy thermometer in pot and cook until temperature reaches 238°. Pour into a 9x13-inch baking dish and let set until hardened. For thicker fudge use a smaller baking dish.

F2T Tip: For chocolate fudge, add 3 tablespoons cocoa. For peanut butter fudge, add 2 tablespoons peanut butter.

Thank You

There is a common theme throughout my book... and my life... which is gratitude. Because I believe we should always live our lives in a state of gratitude, there are a few people I'd like to thank for all their help and support on this magical journey.

To my soulmate and best friend, *Ian*, I am so blessed to have met you. You are one of the most selfless people I know. You are my everything including but not limited to: my photographer, tech guy, web developer, marketing manager, director, producer, wardrobe stylist, taste-tester, food stylist, handyman and sous-chef all while supporting our family. I couldn't have done any of this without you. I wouldn't know where to begin. If we had to hire people to do half of what you've done, we'd have to employ an entire team and the interview process alone would take years! I'm grateful to you

for supporting my dreams and always living by our motto that failure is not an option. You have your own dreams but always put mine first. You keep me motivated even on days where you're exhausted from working all day at the family businesses and on my projects all night. You are my partner in crime... my other half. We are an unstoppable team. From the bottom of my heart I thank you. I couldn't possibly love you more. I love you times a google.

To my *Kaden*, my heart and soul, I am blessed God chose me to be your mommy. You are such a talented, loving, kind and creative soul. I'm so proud of you every day. My dreams have kept me busier than I'd like to be at times but I try to lead by example so the doors of opportunity will be wide open for you. I also want you to see that dreams do come true with hard work and determination. That dimple smile keeps me going even when I'm tired. I love you with all my heart little man... to the moon and stars and California, as we say.

To my family, I couldn't do this thing called life without all of you. My mother, my hero, holds me up while my sister and brother-in-law have my back. How lucky I am to walk through life with you all by my side. The memories we have created together have given me the best material I could ever imagine for my book between traditions, stories and recipes. There's no measure to my love and respect for all of you. It is limitless. It is infinite.

To the *Ritter family*, I thank you letting me do pretty much whatever I want in your markets and never ever questioning me, not even once. I breezed into your lives out of nowhere and started this whole farm to table thing on a whim and a prayer. Your support is more appreciated than you'll ever know and you've given me one of the greatest gifts of all in Ian. I love you all and am honored to be a part of your family.

Finally, last but not certainly not least, I am beyond grateful to my publisher for believing in me and my story enough to make my dream of being an author a reality. What a pleasure this journey has been with the *Great American Publishers family*. Your help and support has been such an incredible blessing to me. What an amazing group of talented professionals I have had the honor to work with in all of you. I've learned so much about an industry in which I know very little. I thank you this wonderful opportunity.

Recipe Index

Cookbooks Make Great Gifts

Great American Publishers makes beautiful cookbooks featuring cherished recipes from hundreds of home cooks across the country. Visit us online for Great American news, bonus recipes, cooking tips, exclusive discounts, and more.

Want to see more?
Call today for a free catalog:
1-888-854-5954

Do you have a retail store? Call for discounts & terms: 1-888-854-5954

www.GreatAmericanPublishers.com
facebook.com/greatamericanpublishers